CW01666049

Copyright (c) 2020 Feyisayo Ojo
All rights reserved. No portion of this book may be reproduced, stored in any retrievable device, transmitted in any form by any means, mechanical electronic, photocopy or otherwise without the written permission of the copyright owner.

All scriptures quoted in this book are from the King James version and a few from Jubile version of the Bible.

Audacity of Praise Copyright @ 2017
Feyisayo Ayodeji Ojo
ISBN - 978-978-979-877-3
January 2020

For all enquiries and purchase order, contact
Lagos:
+234 815 848 0571, +234 803 406 6940
+234 703 076 3545, +234 812 841 1231

Abuja:
+234 803 809 7960, + 234 806 305 8237

Uyo:
+234 902 624 7488

PortHarcourt
+234 803 594 4424

United Kingdom:
+44 7931 614 668, +44 7450 861133

United States
+1 443 535 7311
+1 443 418 0636
Email: hearbeatworshipers@gmail.com

Dedication

... Job 32:8 But [there is] a spirit in man: and the inspiration of the Almighty giveth them understanding.

The breath of the Almighty gave me the inspiration to write this book and for this reason, I dedicate it to Him who is the Giver of Wisdom, the ever-living God who inhabits the praises of His people.

Foreword

The reward of Praising God is inestimable and undoubtedly enormous. The scriptures say that the Lord inhabits the praise of His people; hence, Praise is one thing God cannot do for Himself and requires that we do it for Him.

Audacity of Praise is a unique book, specifically to open our eyes to the benefits of giving praise to the Maker of heaven and earth. It also declares with life realities, illustrations of prayers answered and healing perfected through praise.

By virtue of my position as the Senior Pastor of Life Changers Word Ministry (LCWM) where the author is currently giving his stewardship, I have known him for over two decades and been opportune to have direct contact with him and his enviable commitment to the work of God. He is a man of honour; humble and always with a heart of praise to God.

This book comes highly recommended by me as the information contained in the book serves as an eye-opener to the importance of praise, benefits and the role of Praise in human lives.

Pastor Emmanuel Onimisi Daniels
Senior Pastor (LCWM).

Acknowledgement

There is no me without You Lord and You made me who I am today. I will forever be grateful for your saving grace, the gift of singing and your inspiration upon me to receive and accomplish this project and many more to come. Thank you, the Father of Life!

My very special thanks to Adeola, My FD as we fondly call each other and a wonderful wife of over fifteen years. Truly you are a gift from the Lord; you are not just a great wife, but my best friend next to God and my helper! The mother of our lovely three children – Breakthrough, Divine and Praise. I thank you for your prayers and understanding all the time. Thank you, my love!

To my dearly beloved brother Kennedy Agumanu, your passion and effort in proofreading, correcting all the scripts and bringing the book to a published standard is highly appreciated. You will never lack help and your success in life is not negotiable!

Deaconess Roseline Daniels is a woman with a heart of gold whose aim is to always see vision Fulfilled. Your heart desires shall be granted in Jesus Mighty Name.

I will not fail to acknowledge my childhood friend- Blessing Awoleye, my brother from another mother Oluwakayode Osorun and my wonderful friend - Mrs. Gift Amaugoh George. You all are too wonderful not to be remembered and you are well appreciated for your contributions.

Pastor Olusola Olufayobi has been a great prayer partner and a wonderful minister of God, thank you for your prayers and encouragement all the time and may God enlarge your coast the more in Jesus name Amen.

The prayer of a mother can never be taken for granted. Thank you, my mother, – Gladys Eniyanlola for your sacrifice in all ramifications in my upbringing, God will keep you for me and you shall live long to enjoy the fruits of your labour in Jesus name.

Dear Daddy and Mama Emmanuel O. Daniels, thank you for your humility, backing and encouragement in all that pertains to life and your contributions in the making of a man like me. I cannot help but acknowledge and appreciate your support and effort. You will surely be rewarded in Jesus name.

I appreciate everyone who has been a great inspiration to me, most especially all the great family members of Life Changers Word Ministry Baltimore- Maryland USA, Star City Ikeja Lagos and Life Changers all over the world. Your efforts shall never go unrewarded in Jesus name!

CONTENTS

Introduction

The foundation of everything in this life is the Bible and the Bible is absolutely everything and there can never be an alternative to the Bible. Right from the outset, the old covenant revealed how the whole earth was without form and was shapeless; it, however, took the courageous nature of the Ancient of Days, God Almighty to call forth those things that were not as if they were. Though none of this present generation was on earth to witness the process of creation in that era, God's word and works speak for itself before all today.

Some years back, I climbed and stood on a mountain top where I was privileged to have a perfect view of one of the finest and well topographically structured cities in Nigeria. While the expedition lasted at that particular location in Jos city, I began to imagine the awesomeness of God in creation. I looked into the skies and I could feel His presence, I looked sideways and behold the undulating plains and other elevated lands which could only have been architecturally made by the boldness of God via creation. Subsequently, I discovered that tears were rolling down my face in reverence to the God of creation. Though, I cannot recollect vividly whether I sang a song of worship in appreciation to God or not, but was quietly meditating on the word that says:

"It is only a fool that says there is no God!"

While we continue in this short journey of knowledge sharing on

Audacity of Praise, I wish to underscore that there is no other way of learning the subject and topic of praise if not by action rooted in the courage that the exercise is not in futility. It can only be demonstrated as there is no other way to praise than "to praise". The Bible was inspired and subsequently written via action. Little wonder the book of the Apostles was full of power-packed actions which are a reference point today simply because all their deeds were done in boldness and subsequently documented.

At the point of persecution and torture, the Apostles were so resilient that death was not a threat but a journey of peace and completion to them. Little wonder, it was recorded of Apostle Paul that as long as he lives on earth, it is for Christ and to die is gain.

> ***"And now, Lord, behold their threatenings: and grant unto thy servants, that with all boldness they may speak thy word, By stretching forth thine hand to heal; and that signs and wonders may be done by the name of thy holy child Jesus."***
>
> *Acts 4:29-30*

Have you read the story of Esther? An unequivocal display of audacity! Not minding whose ox is gored. There was a pragmatic display of uncommon boldness which Esther cascaded to a generation that would have simply been enmeshed in disarray if they had not stood their ground against the enemy's death sentence which was systematically passed on the

Jews in the land of Persia. Esther did not just sit on the fence; she acted in faith and boldness. The boldness displayed by Esther was second to none though we may not be dwelling on this as we are embarking on a journey to praise land powered by audacity.

> ***"Go, gather together all the Jews that are present in Shushan, and fast ye for me, and neither eat nor drink three days, night or day: I also and my maidens will fast likewise; and so will I go in unto the king, which is not according to the law: and if I perish, I perish."***
>
> ***Esther 4:16***

I crave your indulgence to permit me to quickly mention the three Hebrews who dare death and shamed timidity. They refused to be convinced against their belief on which God is, they refused to move their body to participate in the dance of shame to a dead god-talk less of paying obeisance to a carved and man-made image.

The reward that probably would have been given to the three Hebrews would have been landed properties in the chosen area, chieftaincy titles and cash rewards. They were rather gloriously rewarded by erecting the altar of His testimony in the land of Babylon via His mighty deeds.

"Shadrach, Meshach, and Abednego answered and said to the king, O Nebuchadnezzar, we are not careful to answer thee in this matter. If it be so, our God whom we serve is able to deliver us from the burning fiery furnace, and he will deliver us out of thine hand, O king. But if not, be it known unto thee, O king, that we will not serve thy gods, nor worship the golden image which thou hast set up."

Daniel 3:16-18

Chapter 1

AUDACITY – AN OVERVIEW

DEFINITION AND ILLUSTRATIONS OF CONCEPTS

AUDACITY

This is an English word with numerous variance and synonyms ranging from simple and contextual meanings. The word Audacity simply means Unconventional, Insolent, Fearlessness, Intrepid, Boldness and Daring which is the most common of all. A lot of Christians have dared God in different ways, while some others have remained outstanding as a result of their tenacity, boldness, and doggedness. These are features every follower of Christ should exhibit in this heavenly raise. As a Christian, we need to be audacious for the task ahead; little wonder Jesus intercepted Paul on his way to persecute Christians in Damascus. Similarly, the audacity of David gave him an opportunity to become outstanding despite his age and position in the family. David has a fearless mind even before he was chosen by God as King "Little wonder he was called A Man after God's own heart" if you read the scriptures well, you will notice that in his exploits and adventures, David had already fought several wild animals dreaded by humans and he defeated them one after the other before going to face Goliath. It is this boldness and fearlessness he uses to defeat Goliath to the amazement of the people and glory to God.

What do we understand by Audacity of Praise?

The weather was relatively cold and a Bible-teaching church in one of the renowned temperate climates of the western countries had given me an invite to speak on praise in one of their church programs. While asking the Holy Spirit for direction and what he would want His people to know more about praise, He suddenly showed up via his inspiration and gave me the word Audacity of Praise. I could not hold back as I stood on my feet and screamed the topic with excitement. I repeatedly held on to the word and sounded it several times while I moved in various directions within the living room. I was so full of appreciation to God for bringing a deeper meaning and understanding of the given topic within a twinkle of an eye. I will conclude on this shortly, but I think it is important to briefly describe what Audacity of Praise is and thereafter take it further.

Audacity is truly all about Boldness, and boldness is the limitless power of God.

Looking at this critically, one of the weapons the devil uses in bowing his victims head is timidity. Audacity according to the dictionary definition is a confident and daring quality that is often seen as shocking or rude: an audacious quality!

The bible says ***"the righteous shall be bold as a lion".*** If timidity which is the opposite of audacity can simply be further interpreted as fearfulness then it is completely against the teachings of the faith as a fearful or doubtful heart can never receive anything from God. In this race of destiny, faith is an essential weapon as the elders of old obtained a bette and excellent report through it. The elders as accounted for in the book of Hebrews became heroes and heroines by virtue of their boldness in decision making and actions by going extra miles above others and gallantly taking great risks for God in so many circumstances.

> ***"Now faith is the substance of things hoped for, the evidence of things not seen, for by it the elders obtained a good report. Through faith, we understand that the worlds were framed by the word of God so that things which are seen were not made of things which do appear."***
> ***Hebrews 11:1-3***

It is impossible to talk about Audacity without its engine room which is **"Faith".**

Faith propels us to work, as it is the substance of things hoped for and the evidence of things not seen. Faith also may not be properly understood without beaming our searchlight on "Fear" as it is a spiritual tool to measure Christian faith. It is assumed that any Christian found or who lives in fear does not have faith and is not qualified for the Christian race. The bible says:"faith without work is dead". Therefore, the relationship between "Faith" and "Fear" is interconnected and heavenly as they cannot be separated successfully. Furthermore, it is worthy of note that fear serves as a check on every Christian faith (The fear of the Lord is the beginning of wisdom ... Proverbs 9vs10). Before we look at the other side of fear, the good thing about it is that it increases our knowledge in God if rightly applied and used in referencing the Creator. It gives a clearer understanding and transparency of God in His very simple and terrific nature. Outside this, the other aspect of fear completely negates the principle of boldness. Fear in the negative sense is a tormentor and has everything it takes to handcuff its victims almost all through the race of life.

I have the leading to quickly pray this for you; by virtue of your contact with this book, I decree that every chain of torment is today broken in your life. I evoke the power of the Holy Ghost to set you free from every plague that fear has caused in your life. You probably may have been a slave to fear, you are today totally delivered in Jesus mighty name Amen!

Entering into His presence and the Holies of Holy takes a bold mind and a prepared heart. The throne of grace is not a place of doubtful mind, but a place a mountain moving and a valley filling heart. It is the starting point for any solution that can ever be obtained in life. It can also be a place of disappointment for the double-minded.

"Let us, therefore, come boldly unto the throne of grace that we may obtain mercy, and find grace to help in time of need." Hebrews 4:16

PRAISE

As earlier mentioned, praise is better thought by action. It is an expression of thanksgiving with a heart of gratitude. A mark of approval for excellent deeds; an accolade to a being for extraordinary performances. The petition that moves God is praise. Praise is the nutrient of God and praise moves

Him from the throne. Permit me to say that the best definition of Praise cannot be found better expatiated as we have it all through the book of Psalms.

Psalm 150 says:
Praise ye the LORD. Praise God in his sanctuary: praise him in the firmament of his power.
Praise him for his mighty acts: praise him according to his excellent greatness.
Praise him with the sound of the trumpet: praise him with the psaltery and harp.
Praise him with the timbrel and dance: praise him with stringed instruments and organs.
Praise him upon the loud cymbals: praise him upon the high sounding cymbals.
Let everything that hath breath praise the LORD. Praise ye the LORD.

Talking about Audacity of Praise, it is the power of boldness backing praise as a sacrifice with numerous wonders following. Seeing praise as a sacrifice delivers its dividends into our hands and we shall be looking at praise as a sacrifice in the next chapter to aid our understanding as made known by the Holy Spirit.

Welcome on board as we explore and embark on this journey of Audacity of Praise together.

Chapter 2

SACRIFICE OF PRAISE

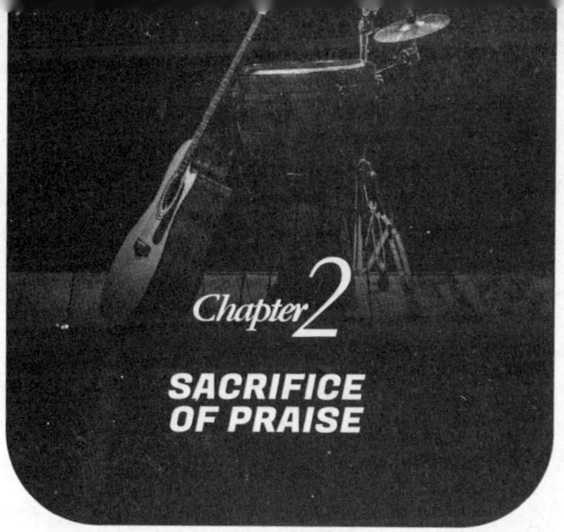

Chapter 2 SACRIFICE OF PRAISE

To say the least, a Praise giver is a man of confidence, boldness, and sacrifice and will be willing to boldly face any circumstance at any given moment. A man of praise is a carrier of sacrifice and could simply be referred to as a risk-taker as praise itself is a sacrifice. Right from the outset, a businessman or an investor who is not willing to take a risk is not ready to make an investment so also a praise giver who is not ready to understand and view praise as a sacrifice is not ready to enter into the business of praise and fully utilize praise as a weapon.

The best teacher and greatest tutor of all ages described praise as a sacrifice. With this tag, praise as a sacrifice has the tendency of building and uprooting and causing untold hardship and wreaking havoc in the camp of evil. Understanding the power surrounding simple praise offered to God can only best be described in its totality as 'audacity of praise'. Praise does not look at faces and crowns, praise as a sacrifice can dare anything and can do anything. Praise is a fire and will not stop burning until it has completely ruined the camp of evil when offered as a sacrifice. The audacity of praise!

If you carefully ponder over the word sacrifice, you will discover that it takes a man with a big heart, someone who is very much ready to give it what it takes to achieve the unusual. A man of sacrifice will damn every consequence and his determination will be if I perish, I perish!

Have you ever witnessed a herbalist or a traditionalist carrying a sacrifice at the wee and dead hours of the night? Despite the fact that they are not of God's kingdom, the seriousness and importance attached to their mission are usually of no little measure. The herbalists have special regalia with a devilish sceptre of authority to make unusual sounds to their gods. They proceed, chanting incantations to accompany the sacrificial offerings in their hand. Let me quickly ask you children of God and how much preparation and how prepared are your heart before you climb the altar of praise? These people have a mission! It is either they are destroying a destiny to raise another destiny, it is either they weakening a kingdom to raise another kingdom, it is either they are collapsing an authority to subsequently reign supreme, it is either they are carrying out one wicked act or the other by reason of their sacrifice.

These people; once determined are unstoppable, but only by reason of the anointing can their mission be halted. Sacrifice to them is a point of connection where their gods are evoked. Sacrifice is the language of errand clearly understood by their gods; hence the importance attached to the assignment.

What then is a Sacrifice of Praise?
I would like us to quickly look at the scriptures

Hebrews 13:15
"By him, therefore, let us offer the sacrifice of praise to God continually, that is, the fruit of our lips giving thanks to his name."

Psalm 50:23 – JUB
"Whosoever sacrifices praise glorifies me, and to him that orders his ways aright I will show the salvation of God."

Romans 12:1
"I beseech you therefore, brethren, by the mercies of God, that ye present your bodies a living sacrifice, holy, acceptable unto God, which is your reasonable service. And be not conformed to this world: but be ye transformed by the renewing of your mind, that ye may prove what is that good, and acceptable, and perfect, will of God."

In my strong opinion, sacrifice is a shift or a movement from the realm of comfort or convenience to that of inconvenience. It is a task painfully rendered in anticipation of a fantastic result. Sacrifice is giving up one's own way and will for the superiority of the divinity.

The Merriam – Webster dictionary defines sacrifice as the act of giving up something that you want to keep especially in order to get or do something else to help someone. An act of killing a person or animal in a religious ceremony as an offering to please a god. The offering of food, objects or the lives of animals to a higher purpose.

Sacrifice may not necessarily mean discipline, but significantly, discipline is a major factor as a backup for a sacrificial life. The first preparation for praise is a sacrifice of our entire body. Living a life void of sin and hypocrisy is a daily preparation that cannot be overemphasized. Paul the apostle admonished the believers to present their bodies as a living sacrifice which must be holy and acceptable to God. Little do praise givers know that the number one requirement for rendering and giving praise as a sacrifice is the sacrifice of the giver first and foremost.

It takes discipline to separate from the world to God as we are not of the world. It takes a life wholly dedicated and pleasing unto God to fully understand that praise is not an ordinary offering but a sacrifice. As we saw earlier, an idol worshipper will always prepare his garment, carry his sacrifice with the mission to either kill or make alive. Significantly, we that have been called out as a chosen generation and a royal priesthood need to daily renew our minds; enter into God's own spiritual laboratory for cross-examination in preparation for our next appearance before the altar of praise with our sacrifice of praise.

Today, as we enter into His sanctuary, among the most visible in the congregation are the choristers which were known in the Old Testament days like the fourth born of the twelve tribes of Israel called Judah which literally means Praise. (Genesis 29:35) The task of lifting the souls of men in songs ministration from the ordinary to the terrestrial realm is their basic and primary responsibility. They are the instruments ordained to draw men closer to God through praise and worship. Bridging the gap of existence between man and his maker is an assignment that heaven has committed to this praise leaders and worshippers.

It, however, seems that the consciousness of outward decoration and maximum attention to fashion in all its ramifications is geometrically eroding the essence of an offering of praise as a sacrifice. Making a piece of melodious music before the throne of grace with a consecrated heart to the congregation of saints is completely different from creating an ordinary sound and noise with exposed cleavages, showing hot legs and opening of the entire body on a podium to entertain the congregation. Without prejudice, looking good and smartly dressed is never a condemnable act, but sacrificing the sacred preparatory moments for praise on the altar of vanity will only make people sing from their mouths without necessarily affecting lives nor having a positive impact in their heart. Men will be in the presence of God, but their heart will be several miles away from the touch of God.

I want us to quickly take a look at this scripture:

> ***"But ye are come unto mount Sion, and unto the city of the living God, the heavenly Jerusalem, and to an innumerable company***

> ***of angels, To the general assembly and church of the firstborn, which are written in heaven, and to God the Judge of all, and to the spirits of just men made perfect, "***
> ***Hebrews 12:22-23.***

Jumping into talking about the sacrifice of praise without the sacrifice of the body of praise givers will be of no value. From the above scriptures, do we understand that it will amount to a disgraceful act to appear in Zion filthy? Our fellowship is primarily to God in the company of so many angels, elders, and other great participants. Can you quickly picture in your heart of a well-planned occasion put in place for important dignitaries? All invitees to the gathering must attend in their best or otherwise will be disallowed from participating in the program. How do you think the garment of the angels and the elders appearing in the special program as co-invitees will look like?

Has it come to stick to our memory that not only physical beings are present in God's sanctuary whenever His creatures are ready to offer Him the fruits of their lips which is our praise? Could you now imagine if an invitee now voluntarily decides to appear before his presence in rags among the innumerable company of other worshipers?

Child of God, an unsanctified heart will appear unprepared before the altar of praise. A Praise giver in rag is a praise leader in sin whose body has not been yielded to God for daily purification because cleanliness is next to godliness (Holiness). He can offer nothing but a strange fire before the altar of the Most High God.

And Nadab and Abihu, the sons of Aaron, took either of them his censer and put fire therein, and put incense thereon, and offered strange fire before the LORD, which he commanded them not. And there went out fire from the LORD and devoured them, and they died before the LORD. Then Moses said unto Aaron, this is it that the LORD spake, saying, I will be sanctified in them that come nigh me, and before all the people I will be glorified. And Aaron held his peace.

Leviticus 10:1-3

"The high time we began to realize that coming to Zion entails proper readiness and cleansing of our heart while presenting our body as a living sacrifice is sacrosanct. The sacrifice that must precede our sacrifice of praise is the sacrifice of our body. Nadab and Abihu played a hanky-panky game before the holy altar and they both received an instant judgment from God who is known as a consuming fire. As important as praise is to God, so also is the cleanliness of the carrier."

As admonished by Paul the Apostle in Romans 12: 1 & 2, the first battle to be won before sending our praise on an errand is that of the body. It clealy indicates that the battle of the body must be won first. If we must be sincere, the performance of a student in any examination is based on his o her readiness and level of preparation. Praise is not something to be offerd under emergency consecration, but a constantly prepared heart with a life that daily radiates the glory of God. It clearly condemned conformity with the worldly standard and condole a continuous renewal and transformation of the mind. A bodily preparation that constantly eschews evil, living up to godly expectations and not living a controversial daily Christian life. We are not talking about a praise giver that constantly gets soaked in lustful desire only to silently repent of these deeds when duty calls. The discipline of the body is relentlessly accepting the wish, way and leading of God himself.

Are you a praise leader, listen to me, the Holy Spirit is through this medium calling you to a perfect understanding of who you are and what you are meant to do before you lead his congregation in carrying that sacrifice. Recognition of the place of grace in the given assignment makes your preparation an easy task. The ace that ensures that the race is run without blemish is nothing but grace. God desires a bridge builder and a fulfiller of purpose; He sees your office as a very sacred one that can perfectly be handled by you at any given time as purposed by heavensand dragging his name in the mud or not totally compliance to His way of life is tantamount to ridiculing the grace of God deposited upon your lifeand remember, God cannot be mocked.

Take a look at our larger society, broaden your view beyond the shoe of Africa to the entire world, it will be very glaring that so many are in the field of gospel music. Probe further; many are gospel artists/entertiners while few are gospel Ministers. To be a minister of the Most High God is to understand the basics and rudiments of getting God involved, abling all preparations before the Holy Spirit, not having the mentality o using

Chapter 3

PRAISE AN INSTRUMENT THAT CRUSHES

Chapter 3

PRAISE AN INSTRUMENT THAT CRUSHES

Praise is an instrument that crushes beyond human comprehension that is why it is believed that with praise enemies have no alternative or escape routes. As we start exploring the sacrificial nature of praise and its ruthlessness in dealing with the enemies, it is appropriate to quickly draw our attention to few nomenclatures of the receiver of praise who is God omnipotent, omniscience, and omnipresence. In my experience and little walk with God, the name that can best explain who God is with the deepest satisfaction from the heart is that which is found in the local dialect of His people and most at times can be very difficult to appropriately interpret in the English language because of its originality and source. The praise and encomiums will flow without any hindrance but with a deep sense of fulfilment.

Have you heard of names such as these?
Owo kenbe rebi ija - Dressed gorgeously to battle
Aja ma jebi eni - Fighter who is not guilty in battle
Olorun awon omo ogun - God of Host
Ato fise ogun ran - Enough to be sent to a battle
Agbanilagbatan - The one that delivers totally

Oro godo ganyin – The word Himself
Chukwu ji ekeni ne – God that hold all the powers
Dike na agha – Mighty man in battle
Onye kewara osimiri uhie – He that parted the Red Sea
Agu bata ohia mgbada agbaa oso – When Lion enters the forest every other animal runs away
Ji ana ahu n'oku o na epu ome – The Yam that is being roasted yet it is germinating
Onye ne emema - God that does good
Anu ana agba egbe o na tan nri - An animal being shot a gun yet it continues to feed. Onye na agbo oria - God the healer
Ubangiji – The Supreme Being
Sariki n Salama – Prince of Peace
Mai Taimako – The Helper
Allah Mai Iko – The Powerful God
Tushen Rai – The Author of Life

Noteworthy is the fact that the name of the Lord cannot be exhausted because it is in millions and no man can know it all. For instance, as I was into worship sometime ago, God said I am the King of all Presidents and the President of all Kings!

What comes to your mind when such names stated above and many more that are not written are mentioned? I see nothing but war and battle-ready God who will quickly put the enemies under your feet. When praise is offered as a sacrifice, God activates a fight from the spirit realm, get ready all His missiles to fight for the deliverance of the praise giver. He ensures our souls escape as a bird out of the snare of the fowler, breaking the trap of the enemy to ensure our complete and total victory. In other words, the God of praise though merciful, is a great fighter, avenging the enemies of His children. If perchance, you come across this book and you have not identified with this God, I encourage you to take a bold step of faith and let Him be your God. By implication, it also means that if you are not for this God you are definitely against His children and this is a very dangerous situation for you as someone who is not with Him or on the Lord's side.

"The name of the Lord is a strong tower: the righteous run into it, and is safe."

Proverbs 18:10

"For it is written, As I live, saith the Lord, every knee shall bow to me, and every tongue shall confess to God."

Romans 14:11

"Wherefore God also hath highly exalted him, and given him a name which is above every name: That at the name of Jesus every knee should bow, of things in heaven, and things in earth, and things under the earth; And that every tongue should confess that Jesus Christ is Lord, to the glory of God the Father."

Philippians 2:9-11

You would agree with me that whenever a God-fearing praise leader is ushering God's people into His presence, His name comes to bear, simply because His name is a mighty and strong tower that saves. God is glorified when His beautiful names are called in readiness for war that praise will eventually accomplish as He rises from the outset. Why call His name? No other reason but because, God is ever-living and whenever anyone calls on His name, He answers. He is forever living and demons cannot but tremble at the mention of His name. Knees of demons and principalities come bowing down and situations begin to hear his voice and not the sound of the one carrying the burden. At His presence, everything obeys!

Praise may seem so stupid in confronting our battles, but it is a weapon that is extremely dangerous for the enemies to handle. With praise there is no option for the enemy than to surrender. If we carefully examine the act of rendering praises to God, one thing you will quickly remember now is that the true praise carriers do not wait for the enemy to strike before it is rendered to God. When praise is given with the right mindset and motive, the enemy is caught unaware and unprepared.

Again, let's look at a scenario here; when the people of the world are trying to project their evil manipulations to silence an opponent, they hardly go about announcing that to the enemy. They rather stay within their closet and invoke series of enchantments and resort to various incantations to get their mission accomplished.

It got to a point in the life of the Israelites that God was eagerly in need of their worship and their praises having spent over four hundred years in the land of Egypt. These people were completely enslaved in a strange land after the death of Joseph with a new Pharaoh on the throne. God continuously demanded just one thing! – Tell Pharaoh that I am in dare need of the praise of my people. Listen to me, your service without sacrifice of praise to God makes you vulnerable. Let us quickly take a look at the following scriptures:

> ***"And I say unto thee, Let my son go, that he may serve me: and if thou refuse to let him go, behold, I will slay thy son, even thy firstborn."***
>
> ***Exodus 4:23***

> ***"And afterward Moses and Aaron went in, and told Pharaoh, Thus saith the LORD God of Israel, Let my people go, that they may hold a feast unto me in the wilderness"***
>
> ***Exodus 5:1***

> ***"And the LORD spake unto Moses, saying, Go in, speak unto Pharaoh King of Egypt that he let the children of Israel go out of his land"***
>
> ***Exodus 6:11***

> ***"And thou shalt say unto him, The LORD God of the Hebrews hath sent me unto thee, saying, Let my people go, that they may serve***

me in the wilderness: and, behold, hitherto thou wouldest not hear.."

Exodus 7:16

"And the LORD spake unto Moses, Go unto Pharaoh, and say unto him, Thus saith the LORD, Let my people go, that they may serve me"

Exodus 8:1

Did you discover anything or notice something in the verses of scriptures highlighted above? There was no moment God did not lay emphasis on that one single request from chapter four to eight of the book of Exodus. "I need my people to serve me" Permit me to say here that God was desperate for praise. He was in need of praise which no other inhabitants of the earth could satisfactorily give to Him during the period. Praise is a pure service to God; it is His food and the very essence of creating man, however, God is complete in Himself. Furthermore, it is obvious that God did not compromise this same request! Can you sit back and have a very deep thought as you ponder on why God refused to change His mind concerning His demand from Pharaoh through Moses and Aaron to release the Israelites to worship Him in the wilderness?

Pharaoh's ignorance and refusal to heed to the need of the God of praise despite repeated warnings and commands to let the people of God proceed on that great mission led to his complete destruction and extermination of himself, family and his warriors. It is important to say at this point that ignoring the instruction of the Lion of the tribe of Judah by Pharaoh was his most foolish decision which was borne out of his pride and arrogance during that period; for this reason was Pharaoh created by God to show the entire world how important praise is to Him.

Let me stress further here that, Pharaoh was completely unaware of the names and personalities of God, (Lesson Point: when God demands praise, He can crush to have it. Please always offer praise whenever, wherever and however He wants it.) If only he knew that he was keeping one of the twelve tribes of Israel known as Judah in bondage along with others, he probably would have had a rethink as JUDAH is specially designated to sing His praise – How then can you cage the praise that belongs to Jehovah God? Pharaoh succeeded successfully in playing with fire, and he was mercilessly burnt beyond attornment. Little Wonder, he lost his son and everything that has ever made him happy in life.

I also need to quickly point your attention to another fatal error committed by Pharaoh. He equated himself with the God that owns the entire universe. He probably felt that the Lord's song could be given in a strange land. God perhaps was not really demonstrating any form of anger for suffering the people all the while; He had his plans, covenants and promises intact for the people of Israel for the appointed time. He needed to train and ensure that he would get quality praise from the elects and have a satisfactory experience from their praise services in the wilderness.

Pharaoh's stupidity was however culminated on the fact that he had the audacity to tamper with the praise that God needed at that crucial time. God took his time to prone, drill and train them in every act and parts of worship while in bondage so as to get the best from them when out of bondage! Pharaoh was however taking this act of God for stupidity and giving God condition and at the same time dictating how the concert in demand by God would be. It was really not his fault, but simply an expression of ignorance of the power of the God of creation.

Take a look at this - Do you realize that the praise and worship requested by God had not yet been offered before the destruction of Pharaoh and his people eventually came to pass? Does that mean anything to you? I am more than convinced that God and the heavens will always rejoice when quality praise is in the pipeline. Can you therefore begin to imagine how much ground God will cover and how far He will go when praise is then wholeheartedly rendered to Him? That Pharaoh would not allow God's people meet Him with their praises made Him furious and would not let Pharaoh go unpunished for denying His people an access to Him.

May I quickly have the attention of Christians and church leaders for a second here; the land of Egypt was like a rehearsal ground for Israelites waiting for the appointed time, it was however like God was neither involved nor aware of their predicaments, but He was very much involved in it. In our local churches, hardly do we have our leaders encouraging and staying by their Levites during times of difficult songs rehearsals knowing well that they are instruments of fight for the entire congregation against the oppression of the devil. God dealt with Pharaoh for tampering with the instruments of His praise.

This may be small compared to the fact that some leaders hardly recognize nor allocate good time for this great assignment. The biggest blunder anyone or any congregation could commit is none recognition of the importance of praise in church programs and the seemingly allocation of intangible time for praise in favour of other church 'activities'. Appearing before the throne of grace for corporate worship is of course recommended in the scripture, creating room for endless praise to God brings about an instant appraisal to raise the giver. In a spirit filled church, what quickly creates an atmosphere for a miracle that makes the cloud to quickly gather by ushering in the holy presence of the Most High God is through the praise given to Him. Via praise, He rises from his throne to honour his people; He creates a lasting experience of his presence and to present His people with undeniable proofs and solutions to their situations.

Yes, it is true that Pharaoh denied God of His praise and place and he was severely punished for it. Can we look at a situation where a son of the kingdom either by act of commission or omission refuses to give God his praise? It is very simple; such a one has given the devil a room and an opportunity to strike without any alternative.

In the land of Egypt, Pharaoh tried all he could to give God an alternative, but God vehemently refused and we can boldly conclude that with praise in place, there is no alternative for the enemy. If the enemy tries all his gimmicks to prevent praise from holding, there is no route of escape for him as God will ruthlessly crush him and if on the other hand, praise still holds, no alternative for the enemy either, other than being made a stepping stone for the praise giver.

Let me close this chapter by comparing your praise with smokes that makes the enemies uncomfortable. When you release your praise, it becomes a sweet smelling savour to God while it becomes a choking smell for the enemy. To force a big rat out of its abode, apply the smoke factor and see what happens within a few minutes of the exercise. Such an animal has no other alternative than to either die inside the hole or struggle out of the hole into the waiting hands of the hunter or death. Your praise is your enchantment, it is your incantation and it is like a smoke that gives no other alternative for the enemy to live. Give it today!

Chapter 4

PRAISE: A COVENANT PRESERVER

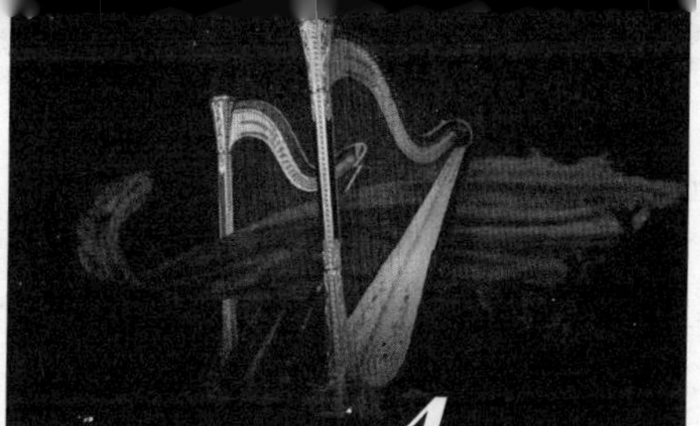

Chapter 4

PRAISE: A COVENANT PRESERVER

Dearest friends, let me start by asking you a question and I would implore that you think deeply before making any attempt to answer. Has God ever lied? I have my own response and may I request that you go along with me as we consider Praise as a Covenant Preserver.

What is Covenant?

Covenant is an oath; it is a seal, a surety and a keeper of promise. It is a gauge that measures integrity! Covenant is God and God is covenant as it involves His name.

> ***"Wherein God, willing more abundantly to shew unto the heirs of promise the immutability of his counsel, confirmed it by an oath: That by two immutable things, in which it was impossible for God to lie, we might have a strong consolation, who have fled for refuge to lay hold upon the hope set before us."***
>
> *Hebrews 6: 17, 18*

I believe the above scripture must have addressed the question raised at the beginning of this chapter. Biblical point of view reveals covenant as an expression of God's unchangeable character and His unwillingness to go back on His covenanted promises. It steadily, expressly and steadfastly defines the uncompromising attitude of God. Various characters in the Bible are proof that when God says, He sees through. Check through the Old Testament – Abraham, Isaac, Jacob to the generation of Joseph at every point in time see the God of Covenant in action. Time is not a constraint, neither is change in time or season a factor that can negate God's covenant. Man may lie, God will ever remain faithful. God said in the scriptures, that He is not a man that He should lie or the son of man that He should repent of His words.

Let us quickly look at the following scriptures of God's promises and covenants with Abraham which was all fulfilled:

> ***"And I will make of thee a great nation, and I will bless thee, and make thy name great; and thou shalt be a blessing"***
>
> ***Genesis 12:2***

> ***"And the LORD said unto Abram, after that Lot was separated from him, Lift up now thine eyes, and look from the place where thou art northward, and southward, favour and eastward, and westward:"***
>
> ***Genesis 13:14***

"And he brought him forth abroad, and said, look now toward heaven, and tell the stars, if thou be able to number them: and he said unto him, so shall thy seed be."
Genesis 15:5

"Neither shall thy name any more be called Abram, but thy name shall be Abraham; for a father of many nations have I made thee."
Genesis 17:5

There was no single promise left unfulfilled. Death is not an obstacle to bringing His words to pass as we saw in the life of the children of Israel after the death of Joseph. God's covenant of deliverance made with Abraham transcended to the generations after Joseph. What a faithful God!

Having established that the God of Praise who daily takes pleasure in our praise and adoration is a God of Covenant, and then you have a great opportunity to present your praise for a covenant relationship with Him. This invariably implies that a giver of praise is a partner with the God of the covenant. Conveniences or inconveniences can never deter or hinder God from keeping any covenant made with Him. This suffices me to say that before we explore this chapter further, another powerful name that differentiates the Most High and the only Great God from all others is that He is a Covenant Keeping God. Can you now see that you have been missing in action by not fully committing God to wonders via your praise by trying to make a covenant with Him in Praise?

> ***"He staggered not at the promise of God through unbelief;***
> ***But was strong in faith, giving glory to God;"***
>
> *Romans 4:20*

Abraham was the father of faith as we all know right from the days of the Bible. He walked with God and exhibited unshakeable faith in Him. Take a look at the above scripture, it was credited to him that he is a giver of glory to God. A man who worships and praises God is simply ascribing glory to Him.

What is Glory?

It may be difficult to describe and define glory as it is God Himself. Glory is God's nature and radiance. Glory is one of His numerous names and the realm of glory is the throne and abode of the most high. His appearance in glory is not just like a devouring fire on the mountain as experienced by Moses and the Israelites, but also the completeness of God apart from being a supernatural characteristic. One of the best and simplest ways of giving glory to God is unblemishly appearing before His altar to worship and sing His praise which we have just been told that Abraham did continually.

> ***"You are worthy, O Lord, to receive glory and honor and power: for you have created all things, and for your pleasure they are and were created."***
>
> ***Revelation 4:11***

> ***"And the four and twenty elders and the four beasts fell down and worshipped God that sat on the throne, saying, Amen; Alleluia."***
>
> ***Revelation 19:4***

The elders in the book of Revelation right from the days of the Bible have been speechless and still astonished as they have not finished singing all the verses of the hymn of Glory. It has been very difficult to finish up the song as they daily cast their crowns to the glorious God shouting GLORY! GLORY! GLORY!

Friend, can you see God in His Majesty? His glory propels you to release yourself, shed tears and roll before Him in worship like the angels and the elders of old.

If Abraham was a giver of glory, the one who sang His praise and bowed at His feet, then, can anyone put forward a strong justification or reason God should not have preserved and fulfilled the covenant He made with Abraham?? The more the glory you ascribed to God, the better your tomorrow as it cannot but be settled by covenant of praise.

This chapter will be incomplete without taking into cognizance the battle and the victory of the children of Israel over Jericho. When immediately after the victory of the Israelites over the stronghold of Jericho where the walls of Jericho fell down flat, a curse was laid.

> ***"And Joshua charged them at that time, saying, cursed be the man before the LORD, that rises up and builds this city Jericho: he shall lay the foundation thereof with his firstborn, and with his youngest son shall he set up the gates of it."***
>
> ***Joshua 6:26***

Hardly can anything happen in this life without sacrifice. The beginning of an individual may be small as confirmed by the word of God in Job chapter 8:7, but with sacrifice, the latter end will always be better off. Word of wisdom and prophecies may come concerning an individual or a situation; it takes doggedness and fighting spirit to bring spoken words to reality and manifestation. It is important to say that praise is a weapon for fighting and a serious minded Christian will always want to use it judiciously.

> ***"Now Jericho was straightly shut up because of the children of Israel: none went out, and none came in. And the Lord said unto Joshua, See, I have given into thine hand Jericho, and the king thereof, and the mighty men of valour."***
>
> ***Joshua 6: 1, 2***

Joshua was assured of victory right from the moment of preparation for the battle of songs, shout and praise against Jericho. He never relented despite the assurance of God's backing but went ahead to adequately organize and fine tune the takeover process of Jericho. Before we go further, let me ask you this question; right in your closet or while appearing along with other Christians, what have you as an instrument of praise? While you purse and ponder with your mind running through the four corners of your room and heart innocently searching to at least have one to show forth, we shall have a better understanding of what instruments of praise are in chapter nine of this book and see the importance of all our tools of praise known as musical instruments.

The walls of Jericho was locked down and straightly shut up, yet it was never a discouragement to Joshua as he prepared himself, the people and the priests as well. He specifically instructed and handed down to everyone the best strategy and approach as instructed by God for the battle.

The real action started when the appointed season finally came; a seven day victorious rally commenced with thirteen times of glorious match round the city. The victory was finally attained and the gates that were locked were finally made open by heavenly backing.

I have a leading in my spirit to declare and prophesy into your life that henceforth, "You shall not sing His praise in vain. Doors may have been shut against you and your foundation messed up, listen to me as you set

aside the next three days and three nights to seek the face of the Lord not to pray, but praise Him, every shut door shall be opened and every wall of Jericho caging your glory shall crumble in the mighty name of Jesus."
Be ready to return all the glory to God Almighty with a great testimony because your celebration is on the way!

The covenant or vow made to get a task accomplished coupled with the psychological trauma and physical effects of fighting any battle at any time could be far reaching. These acts are more than enough to propel those involved to come up with pronunciations that are either born out of jubilation or provocation which are customarily binding, most especially when life is involved. The case of Jephthah in the book of Judges Chapter 11 is a good example of this illustration.

What did Joshua do after his victory over Jericho?

Pains and bitterness of war become forgotten with the sweetness of victory. Joshua was however not carried away for completely winning the battle as he rode on the wings of victory to seal the future against any unanticipated battle in the land of Jericho.
Joshua rode on the wings of praise, made an oath to seal Israelites victory over Jericho for the present and the future.

> ***"And Joshua adjured them at that time, saying, cursed be the man before the Lord, that riseth up and buildeth this city Jericho: he shall lay the foundation thereof in his firstborn, and in his youngest son shall he set***

> ***up the gates of it. So the Lord was with Joshua; and his fame was noised throughout the country."***
> ***Joshua 6:26***

Joshua's action was not unconnected with the seven days of warfare and victory made by the God who owns our praise. He laid a covenant inform of a curse to preserve the victory attained. If for any reason the victory will be upturned by anyone in the near future, it will not be without a sacrifice of human blood! Several times I have witnessed an uninterrupted worship and praise sessions after which God will gloriously manifest and instruct an individual to present an open cheque inform of request before Him. In times like this, praise offered to God is like a covenant to seal and preserve any request placed before God. In I Kings chapter 16, the future finally came and the enemy tried the God of Joshua with an attempt to build the wall of Jericho which was brought down by the shout of praise. The reign of Ahab in Israel with his wife Jezebel was so terrible that idolatry completely silenced the songs and worship that was meant for God.

> ***"And Ahab the son of Omri did evil in the sight of the Lord above all that were before him. And it came to pass, as if it had been a light thing for him to walk in the sins of Jeroboam the son of Nebat, that he took to wife Jezebel the daughter of Ethbaal king of the Zidonians, and went and served Baal, and***

> ***worshipped him. And he reared up an altar for Baal in the house of Baal, which he had built in Samaria. And Ahab made a grove; and Ahab did more to provoke the Lord God of Israel to anger than all the kings of Israel that were before him."***
>
> ***I Kings 16***

It was during his reign that Hiel started the process of rebuilding the wall of Jericho out of complete disobedience to the God of the covenant. What eventually happened to Hiel?

> ***"In his days did Hiel the Bethelite build Jericho: he laid the foundation thereof in Abiram his firstborn, and set up the gates thereof in his youngest son Segub, according to the word of the Lord, which he spoke of by Joshua the son of Nun."***
>
> ***I Kings 16:34***

As we conclude on this chapter, the above Bible passage is more than strong enough to convince us of the power of covenant via praise. Sign on for His praise today and enter into a covenant of divine preference and preservation for tomorrow.

Chapter 5

PRAISE AS WALL OF DEFENSE

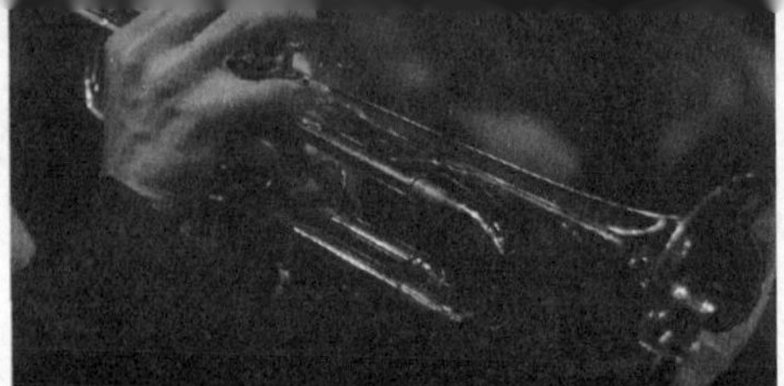

Chapter 5

PRAISE AS WALL OF DEFENSE

Are you accustomed to international borders, most especially those countries with proximity and within the same geographical locations? You will realize that crossing from one country to another involves a clearance from immigration and the security agents at the borders. Aimed at security reasons, walls could be built to help in the restriction of unauthorized movements and to make the work of enforcement officers easy for them. A wall as defined by a meristem dictionary is a high thick masonry structure forming a long rampart or an enclosure chiefly for defence. The illustration to follow quickly crossed my mind as this chapter of Audacity of Praise is being written. In the United States of America, the administration of President Donald Trump seems very much interested in building a strong wall between the border of the United States of America and Mexico. His reasons as proposed among others are for security and protection of the American citizens from unwanted and undocumented fellows though this is not without a political undertone and the final approval for funding can only come from the Legislature arm. The fact, however, remains that when a wall is raised anywhere, the ease of passage is blocked, and it may take permission before anyone can achieve her mission of crossing over.

Can you visualize your Praise as a Wall Of Defense? If a wall is built for defensive purposes, praise offered to God is an invisible wall, much thicker than an ordinary wall. Your praise is a wall of fire that the enemy cannot penetrate if the enemy makes any attempt, the consequences can only be imagined but not prayed for. Let us quickly look at the three Hebrews before king Nebuchadnezzar in the land of Babylon – Hananiah was known as Shadrach, Mishael was given the name Meshach and Azariah was called Abed-Nego. These Generals were in good standing; they lived their lives uprightly before God and raised His banner of righteousness. Just like the natives, they were mandated to offer praise to the gods of the land and this was totally strange and completely contradictory to their upbringings as worshippers of the Most High God. The same sets of instruments of praise needed to praise the King of all Kings were also displayed for the same purposes but to a strange god.

Daniel 3:12-18

"But there are some Jews whom you have set over the affairs of the province of Babylon- Shadrach, Meshach and Abednego-who pay no attention to you, Your Majesty. They neither serve your gods nor worship the image of gold you have set up."

Furious with rage, Nebuchadnezzar summoned Shadrach, Meshach, and Abednego. So these men were brought before the king, and Nebuchadnezzar said to them, "Is it true, Shadrach, Meshach, and Abednego, that you do not serve my gods or worship the image of gold I have set up? Now when you hear the sound of the horn, flute, zither, lyre, harp, pipe and all kinds of music, if you are ready to fall down and worship the image I made, very good. But if you do not worship it, you will be thrown immediately into a blazing furnace. Then what god will be able to rescue you from my hand?" Shadrach, Meshach and Abednego replied to him, "King Nebuchadnezzar, we do not need to defend ourselves before you in this matter. If we are thrown into the blazing furnace, the God we serve is able to deliver us from it, and he will deliver us from Your Majesty's hand. 18 But even if he does not, we want you to know, Your Majesty, that we will not serve your gods or worship the image of gold you have set up.

The battle of supremacy began! An instruction with threats and penalties were simultaneously issued depicting the seriousness of the matter. The heathens offered their praises and bowed to the god of Nebuchadnezzar, but the three Hebrews would not carry out such an abominable act against their God. I have a strong conviction that while this was going on, the songs of praise and adoration to the God of heavens were quietly going through their minds. They were soaked with the praise and worship of the great God in their heart and this busted with authoritative words from their mouths that their Hallelujah belongs to God and not to an ordinary image. They made it clear that God's sacred songs cannot be sung before a wretched and a speechless image of human creation.

As this was ongoing, God was busy converting the fiery furnace of fire of the enemy to a wall of defence for these Heroes of faith. They continued with their worship in their heart to the Giver of life and owner of everything, and were bold enough to confront the king and his agents to do their worst as they would never compromise their faith. They were eventually thrown into the heated furnace, but miraculously happened as not only did the fire turn to a wall of defense, the owner of praise physically came down as a special guest to take over the contest. It is important to say that with your praise, angels are bypassed and God directly takes charge. If God is there for you, it means that the Rock of Ages is physically in action and He becomes a wall of protection that the enemies can never penetrate. For the three Hebrews, power changed hands, a fiery furnace and heated fire became cool air conditioning of protection from the heat of evil prepared by haters of God.

Listen to me, every single day handed over to man by God comprises of so many journeys. You are either voluntarily embarking on these hundreds of metres, kilometres or miles journeys per day or involuntarily doing so. A voluntary journey could be like walking on the way, sporting activities, driving or using other means of transportation. Your involuntary journeys may probably be due to call of nature like sleeping and waking up and many others are all still classified as journeys. Nonetheless, the truth of the matter is that every single time must be redeemed as the day in which all these journeys are embedded is full of evils. When I have the time to release my praise to God, I have a deep sense of divine security with a wall of defence all around me. In ensuring God's wall of defence all around us, we must offer Him sacrifices of praise before the altar of grace.

Interestingly, walls are also built by the enemies for protection and fortification all around themselves. Enemies build physical walls of security while believers via wisdom build spiritual and defensive walls by their praises to God.

Isaiah 25:1-4

1. O LORD, thou art my God; I will exalt thee, I will praise thy name; for thou hast done wonderful things; thy counsels of old are faithfulness and truth.

2. For thou hast made of a city an heap; of a defenced city a ruin: a palace of strangers to be no city; it shall never be built.

3. Therefore shall the strong people glorify thee, the city of the terrible nations shall fear thee.

4. For thou hast been a strength to the poor, a strength to the needy in his distress, a refuge from the storm, a shadow from the heat, when the blast of the terrible ones is as a storm against the wall.

In the context of considering Praise as a Wall of Defense, praises offered to God by His Children protect and preserve, it destroys and exposes the walls built by the enemies. Praise has the capability of turning a built city into a heap and a palace into a ruin. It brings the efforts of strangers into futility, disallowing them from building a city or achieving anything meaningful against God's elect. When all their efforts are uncoordinated, and their roots are deprived of penetrating and reaching a zone of comfort with their foundation broken; praise is smartly releasing devastating blows on the enemies. If believers understand the extent of their powers using praise, they will fight less and their strength will be preserved for praise. Battles will be won, walls will collapse, forces of evil will be exposed, and great battles will be fought and won while they hold their peace. If God withdraws his wall of protection against anyone, such in no distant time is made to face the consequences. No matter how inspiring and melodious his music may be in the sight of God, it becomes an abomination. At a point, King David, the praise maker realized this and had to go back to the basics and was inspired to right his wrongs in Psalm 51. He made a request that God should open his lips so that his mouth could render a genuine praise to Him. He needed to be reassured that the wall of God's divine security is rebuilt all around him so he might not fall victim to the enemy.

As we live daily, our lives must be an extension and expression of His grace. The race of life becomes worthless and dangerous without genuine songs of praise from our heart and we become vulnerable in the hands of the devil and all his cohorts. There is a question that everyone needs to answer - To daily sing His praise and earn God's credit or to daily credit the account of the devil and live in debt? Which is better?

In verse one of Isaiah Chapter 25, there is a personal reference to the great God with a declaration to exalt and worship Him. To Exalt God is to proclaim the glorious honour of His Majesty, to extol the exceeding riches of His grace, to magnify the superiority of His Excellency, to celebrate with a loving gratitude of His wonderful kindness and to see Him as the only Chariots of Fire who surrounded Elijah and His servants, but blinded and humiliated the host of Syrians who were the enemies of His people. I make a declaration and prophesy to your life that as you give God His praise, all your mockers shall be humiliated and displaced in Jesus name! Amen!

How does God appear as a wall of defence? A praise giver moves God to arise from His throne and the enemy of a giver of praise automatically becomes the enemy of God. He appears as a consuming fire to anyone who provokes His fire and a wall of defence to those who ignite the fire of His worship and praise. He becomes a solid rock of defence to those who find offence in the Praise-Giver.

May I clearly say that the existence of mankind is on the insistence of God; it only takes His abiding presence to overcome all evil machinations and insurgencies of the enemies daily orchestrated and put in place because of you. There is no amount of insurance premiums you can daily pay to the treasury of heavens that can ever be compared to the praise God requires of you to earn the daily assurance of His guidance.

Finally, let me ask, have you ever seen a builder whose interest is to have an uncompleted building or abandon his structure halfway? Your response I believe will be in the affirmative. It will amount to waste of resources and effort in futility to have a project abandoned when the means of getting the job done is available.

Listen to this, you are a praise instrument in the hands of God and your praise guarantees a complete and total security of God upon you and your household. Just as a building is meant to shield and protect individuals from harsh and unfavourable situations, so is your praise! Do not stop building a wall of defense with your praise and the more you give it to Him, the more the building is expanding and the more rooms you are creating for a better security for yourself and those around you.

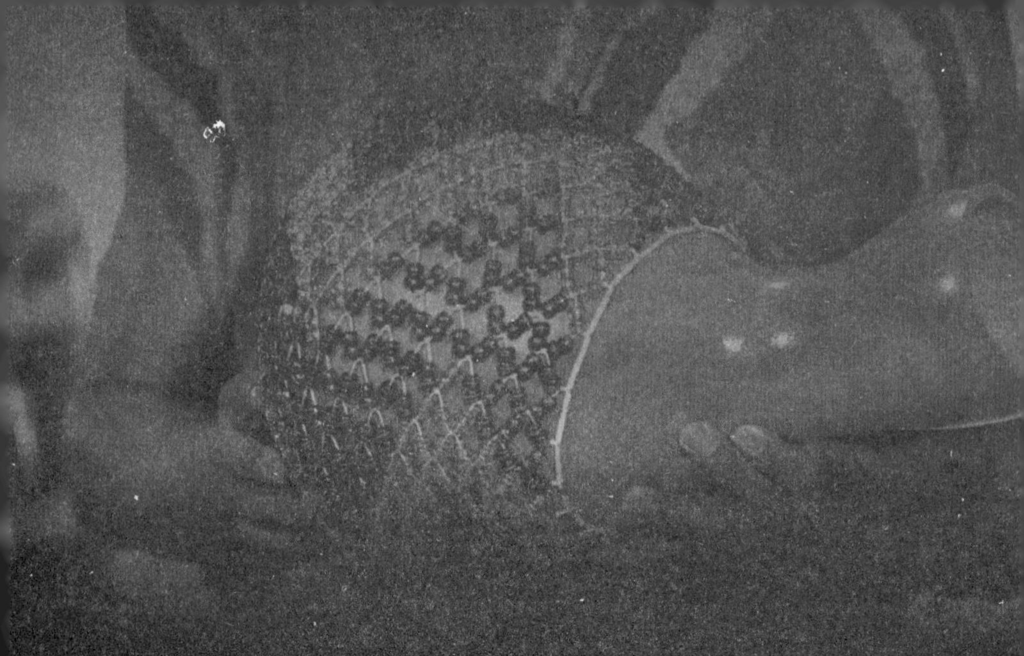

Chapter 6

PRAISE AS A RESTORER

Chapter 6

PRAISE AS A RESTORER

There will always be a test before testimony and if there is no loss, there may not be a restoration or recovery. A man who perfectly fits into this description was Job. In Bible history, Job was an icon of worship. There is the need to quickly look at the resume of Brother Job for a clearer understanding of who he was and stood for.

> ***"There was a man in the land of Uz, whose name was Job; and that man was perfect and upright, and one that feared God, and eschewed evil. And there were born unto him seven sons and three daughters. His substance also was seven thousand sheep and three thousand camels, and five hundred yoke of oxen, and five hundred she asses, and a very great household; so that this man was the greatest of all the men of the east." Job 1:1-3***

Based on Biblical facts, we cannot dispute the following attributes and qualities of the life of Job.

He was a perfect and upright man who feared God and hated sin
He was blessed with a faithful wife and ten children apart from being famous and had tremendous wealth in business.

The moment of Job's test and examination came to pass. Interestingly, on the request of Satan, God gave him the permission to thoroughly examine Job as the Chief Examiner. God is a defender of those that consistently sing His praise and worship Him. He knows the end from the beginning and the power to determine and put individuality to test with an expected result is not hidden from Him.

God cannot vouch for a man whose ways are perverse and inconsistent. To my understanding from the attributes of Job, a man whom God will recommend and can trust will be a man with an in-depth heart of praise and a sincere heart of worship. God must have carefully checked and looked through the praise record of Job for him to have earned God's vote of credibility and confidence. It suffices to say that the consistency of your record of praise to God has the power to boost your mark of approval before Him. He searches the heart and tests the mind to give to every individual according to their ways and deeds. There are hit and run Christians who are always interested in the blessings and take off like the prodigal son. They only dance when fish and bread are available and take off when spiritual exercise comes calling.

How do you know a true friend? He sticks and shows tremendous love and care during a trying period. The time of test came, Job was subjected to all sorts of trials and this happens to be the centre of our discussion in this chapter. What really befell job?

> ***"For the thing which I greatly feared comes upon me, and that which I was afraid of is come unto me. I was not in safety, neither had I rest, neither was I quiet, yet trouble came."***
>
> ***Job 3:25-26 King James Version (KJV)***

Disaster took over the life of Job and there was a loss of 1,000 Oxen, 500 Asses, lightning storms killed his entire 7000 Sheep, Chaldeans stole 3000 Camels from him and lost four of his servants along with all the farmlands.
Tornado killed all his ten children
He had a loss of health
He lost the support of his wife as she wished to die.

What we are interested in looking at here is the response of Job. He made a great choice, a choice of worship even when he was in great pain, when he was alone, when others deserted him, when he could not make ends meet, when friends were not supportive, when his world was shattered and turned upside down, he made a choice to stick to God and still acknowledge him when he drank tears of sorrow like water, he stood and held on to God, he looked up to God, he was near the point of death, he was rebuked, he was attacked and I am sure he was called a great fool for God, but he made a choice of standing and looking unto God.

We are daily confronted with pleasant and unpleasant situations and the power of choice making daily stairs us in the face. There were many options and choices readily available for Job through daily counsel from his friends and the severity of the situation he confronted, but the power of his worship to God constrained him from committing suicide or stop believing God. The power of worship sealed his tongue from saying evil, but to worship God. Worship constrained him from giving up, despite the gravity of his disaster, he strongly believed in God's immunity through his worship.

Have we realized that Job was also a man like us? There is a purpose while this is coming your way today; the praise and worship that God desires of you cannot be given by any other but you. The record of praise that God is interested in to assess you cannot be swapped with someone else's record. The recommendation of heaven on your level of praise is not subjected to any conclusion drawn from the DNA of someone closely related to you, but that of yours.

On a daily basis, so many simple tests that cannot be compared to the misfortune that befell Job come our way. We are faced with simple or major delays at traffic light junctions; we are challenged with the battle of patience at the home fronts. The stress at the workplace and non-friendly environment is a daily reality. The trouble of getting simple tasks accomplished at government parastatals and the uncertainty of honouring appointments and agreements is a constant routine. What can we say of the difficult terrain of getting business done and the policy of the government? Frustration here, frustration there and the uncertainty of what to do next? What is your choice? The answer is for individuals to choose, but Job made a choice of worshipping in a more tense and difficult situation.

In February 2001, I was involved in a ghastly motor accident along Lafia – Makurdi road in Nassarawa state located in the middle belt region of Nigeria, West Africa. It was such a terrible experience that someone thought I had died as he testified after several days of occurrence. The last word I had registered in my memory as the accident occurred was "I shall not die but live to ….. " The sound of the siren blew through my unconscious mind till my eyes were opened and saw myself in a pool of blood while on the way to the hospital. The Federal Road Safety Officials carried me on their hands in the vehicle and the first word that came out of my mouth was a funny question I asked - What happened?

At the hospital, first aid was administered during the day, and this was followed by a phase of pains at the dead of the night. It was a place of loneliness without any family members or acquaintances. It was a point described by the Psalmist as the valley of the shadow of death. Sitting and standing were never the desired positions; neither was sleeping the best option either as a result of the excruciating pains from broken bone, pierced body, wounded face and several cuts. I came to a point of decision making. Could my choice of words be positive or negative amidst my agony? Could I still say God is good and that His mercies endure forever?

Eventually, I made a choice! I summoned the courage to think of His faithfulness. I thought of God's loving-kindness and His counsel of old.

His breath kept me and never allowed death to close its teeth on me. I remembered several thousands of other journeys across the length and breadth of all the geopolitical zones in Nigeria and how He kept me. Most of the journeys were meant for the furtherance of the gospel of Christ at the Nigerian tertiary institutions where Christ Ambassador Students Outreach Fellowships (CASOR) were in existence and where His praise was sung. He made His grace available for me to carry out the assignment as the National Vice President of the body and I could not be less thankful to Him. Grace paved the way to be back in Jos town for proper attention where I had my uncle and his wife.

Yes! I made a choice, I whispered to God in my state of helplessness when my strength was gone. I requested for a new garment of grace for praise, I pledged to renew my worship and never relent in my kingdom service. I said, Oh Lord, this pain is much, please heal me fast so that I can do more of your praise! It was a very short and simple prayer from a heart that craved for more of God but in pains. The result came like a dream; the restorer of everything did the miracle. The head that got pulled off resurfaced with hair within a week and the bruises on the face gradually faded off. I had a figure of eight splints to correct the broken bone and God touched the health professionals to do the right thing at the right time. The testimony came like a dream, my uncle's wife who was in tears the day I got back to Jos praised God for quick healing and restoration of health after a week. During the terrible pains, though the strength to worship and singing praises was completely gone, but a heart of praise was rebirth and reactivated. When God sees a potential praise giver, He will always go out of His way to ensure a divine restoration! Indeed praise is a restorer!

Halleluyah! Job was restored!

> *And the Lord turned the captivity of Job, when he prayed for his friends: also, the Lord gave Job twice as much as he had before. Then came there unto him all his brethren, and all his sisters, and all they that had been of his acquaintance before and did eat bread with him in his house: and they bemoaned him, and comforted him over all the evil that the Lord had brought upon him: every man also gave him a piece of money, and everyone an earring of gold. So the Lord blessed the latter end of Job more than his beginning: for he had fourteen thousand sheep, and six thousand camels, and a thousand yoke of oxen, and a thousand she asses. He also had seven sons and three daughters. And he called the name of the first, Jemima; and the name of the second, Kezia; and the name of the third, Kerenhappuch. And in all the land were no women found so fair as the daughters of Job: and their father gave them inheritance among their brethren. After this lived Job an*

hundred and forty years, and saw his sons, and his sons' sons, even four generations.
Job 42:10-16

Today, the restoration of Job is a point of reference as the scripture was written and became an encouragement to several thousands of people after his death. Praise will never leave you at the same position where you recognized it but take you to a better and higher position. The beginning of Job was small, but praise made his later end greater. God restored double of almost all his losses with a long life in comfort.

Restoration is taking back all that you have lost. Praise ensures that the originality of God is not exchanged in your life for the fake of the devil. If you know how to praise Him, the Almighty God will daily restore your blessings and glory. Though God allowed the devil to examine Job, but the devil was defeated and after all that Job went through, he had his joy restored at the end.

Chapter 7

INFLUENCING NATURE OF PRAISE

Chapter 7

INFLUENCING NATURE OF PRAISE

PRAISE – AS AN INFLUENCER OF THE THRONE OF JUDGEMENT

The nature of Praise is inexhaustible as such in this chapter; attention shall be on Praise as an Influencer of The Throne of Judgement. Throne is a special seat reserved for a monarch. The highest throne ever is not the one occupied by the first-class kings or the most powerful presidents on earth, but the one occupied by the one who is the King of all Presidents and the President of all the Kings – The Almighty God. In a palace or a country, there can only be one King and a president and if for any reason a visitor cannot identify the king in a palace or a president among several officials, the seat is a unique form of identity.

> ***"Where the word of a king is, there is power; And who may say to him, "What are you doing?"***
>
> ***Ecclesiastes 8:4***

The throne of grace where God sits is also a throne of judgment and can never be compared with that of man who is the work of His hands. The word that comes forth and the voice that echoes from this throne is irresistible and incomparable and this is better understood as described by the Psalmist in Chapter 29 of the book of Psalms. The voice from this throne can make or mar any destiny as it is powerful and full of majesty. The voice divides a flame of fire, it breaks the cedars of Lebanon and shakes the wilderness of Kadesh; it has the capability of stripping the forest bare and without doubt, has everything it takes to acquit and sentence a man at his own will without any permission from anyone as He remains God all by Himself!

"And they sung as it were a new song before the throne, and before the four beasts, and the elders: and no man could learn that song but the hundred and forty and four thousand, which were redeemed from the earth."

Revelation 14:3

"God reigneth over the heathen: God sitteth upon the throne of his holiness."

Psalm 47:8

"And after these things I heard a great voice of much people in heaven, saying, Alleluia; Salvation, and glory, and honour, and power, unto the Lord our God: For true and righteous [are] his judgments: for he hath judged the great whore, which did corrupt the earth with

her fornication, and hath avenged the blood of his servants at her hand. And again they said, Alleluia. And her smoke rose up for ever and ever. And the four and twenty elders and the four beasts fell down and worshipped God that sat on the throne, saying, Amen; Alleluia. ..... And a voice came out of the throne, saying, Praise our God, all ye his servants, and ye that fear him, both small and great. And I heard as it were the voice of a great multitude, and as the voice of many waters, and as the voice of mighty thunderings, saying, Alleluia: for the Lord God omnipotent reigneth."

Revelation 19:1-3, 5-6

The throne is a place of authority and power, a place of majesty, justice and honour. Decisions from the throne have great respect for the praise and worship from the pure heart of believers. The throne is a place of holiness, purity and a place of grace. The power that prominently influences the decision from the throne of God is the praise of His worthy servants. Can you imagine a sound of praise from the heart followed by a prayer of judgement upon the enemies? Such an enemy can never escape the judgement from the throne.

Furthermore, we shall shortly be looking at the accounts of King Jehoshaphat in second Chronicles chapter 20. I like to say that Praises and

Calvary worship given to God is like speaking in an unknown language to the hearing of the devil and it shatters and weakens his power. In the time past, the Holy Spirit gave me an illustration and understanding with an in-depth meaning of what it means when we speak in tongues to communicate with God whenever the devil comes accusing us before the throne of grace. It becomes a throne of grace to heirs of His inheritance, while it is a throne of verdict to sentencing the accusers of believers who stand right before God and in awe of His worship and praise.

The illustration goes thus: The Devil being the litigator had succeeded in laying accusations against a believer, I visualized that God would be interested in hearing from the accused as an impartial judge and in the spirit of fairness. God asked the accused to state his own side of the case. The believer who is the accused, rather than respond to God in the normal language well understood by the devil, defended himself by speaking in an unknown tongue that the devil could not comprehend. God, in turn, faces the complainer, the devil to fault or argue against what the believer stated as his defence. At this point, the devil responded by saying ... how do you expect me to know when I could not pick anything from all that the accused said. God responded and said if that is the situation; it will be difficult to prosecute the case further since you lack understanding of the language used by the believer... Case dismissed!

The Devil and his cohorts lack understanding when it comes to the language of praise and the more reason while a praise maker is a dangerous fellow to the gathering of the devil and his agents of darkness. Praise lightens every darkness and the wicked ones cannot stand in the territory of praise; while the devil keeps one in shackles and bondage, praise breaks chains and set loose. The enemy enslaved and caged Paul and Silas in prison, but praise made their freedom possible without any negotiation with the criminals and agents that locked them up.

King Jehoshaphat had a remarkable experience in praise giving to God that can never be erased in the history of the Bible. Follow me through as we examine the Audacity, the Power and the Influence of the Praise of God's people as it levelled, exterminated and permanently silenced the enemies of Judah.

> ***"And now, behold, the children of Ammon and Moab and mount Seir, whom thou wouldest not let Israel invade when they came out of the land of Egypt, but they turned from them and destroyed them not;***
> ***Behold, I say, how they reward us, to come to cast us out of thy possession, which thou hast given us to inherit.***
> ***O our God wilt thou not judge them? For we have no might against this great company that cometh against us; neither know we what to do: but our eyes are upon thee."***
>
> ***2 Chronicles 20:10-12***

Daniel confidently proclaimed in the Bible that if you know the Lord your God, you shall be strong and do exploits. Jehoshaphat, the king of Judah was challenged by the Moabites and Ammonites along with their supporters. The fear of the pending battle humbled him to seek the face of God by proclaiming a fast throughout the land. He reported the enemies to God and as well inquire on what to do. Listen to me, when the enemy is out to attack, it is not just out to steal by taking away your inheritance or destroy, but to kill and ultimately terminate the essence of your living which is to give God your praise and worship. Jehoshaphat demanded for the judgement of God upon these enemies as their target was the mighty instruments of God's praise being challenged.

There is a force that moves the throne of judgment without any resistance and it is this same force that serves as a catalyst for the throne to respond without delay. Jehoshaphat sought the face of God and asked for His judgement. He was very much aware that the God of Abraham and the Israelites sit on the same throne. Jehoshaphat was humbled enough to pray before making any move, express total confidence and reliance on God, while the enemies depended on physical weapons of war. Praise by another meaning is, therefore, a judgement upon the enemies and victory in advance before the real battle commences.

> ***Ye shall not need to fight in this battle: set yourselves, stand ye still, and see the salvation of the Lord with you, O Judah and Jerusalem: fear not, nor be dismayed; tomorrow go out against them: for the Lord will be with you. And Jehoshaphat bowed his head with his face to the ground: and all Judah and the***

inhabitants of Jerusalem fell before the Lord, worshipping the Lord. And the Levites, of the children of the Kohathites, and of the children of the Korhites, stood up to praise the Lord God of Israel with a loud voice on high.
And they rose early in the morning, and went forth into the wilderness of Tekoa: and as they went forth, Jehoshaphat stood and said, Hear me, O Judah, and ye inhabitants of Jerusalem; Believe in the Lord your God, so shall ye be established; believe his prophets, so shall ye prosper.
And when he had consulted with the people, he appointed singers unto the Lord, and that should praise the beauty of holiness, as they went out before the army, and to say, Praise the Lord; for his mercy endureth forever. And when they began to sing and to praise, the Lord set ambushments against the children of Ammon, Moab, and mount Seir, which were come against Judah; and they were smitten.

2 Chronicles 20:17- 22

God gave a very simple instruction to Jehoshaphat, “prepare my praise; I will do the fight”. The children of Judah, Jerusalem and the Levites of Korhites gathered instruments of praise as against the enemy’s physical artilleries of destruction; they proceeded to the battle front. They so much

Black

believed in the God of their fathers and that their praises will move God to action on the throne as boldly declared by Jehoshaphat.
In everything we do leadership matters as it is sometimes difficult for the faith and strength of followers and subordinates to be bigger or higher than that of the leader. In this case, praise was a serious business to Jehoshaphat that the organization was second to none with various responsibilities given to different sets.

The praise and worship of Judah ascended and influenced the throne of grace to send immediate judgement upon the enemies. The enemies made real their threat as they gradually and ignorantly advanced to battle the people of Judah. God's action became visible as the Ammonites battled the Amorites and killed one another. In turn, the soldiers were all completely exterminated while the throne of judgement commanded their self-destruction.

> ***"So when Judah came to a place overlooking the wilderness, they looked toward the multitude; and there were their dead bodies, fallen on the earth. No one had escaped."***
>
> ***"When Jehoshaphat and his people came to take away their spoil, they found among them an abundance of valuables on the dead bodies, and precious jewellery, which they stripped off for themselves, more than they could carry away; and they were three days***

gathering the spoil because there was so much. And on the fourth day they assembled in the Valley of Berachah, for there they blessed the Lord; therefore the name of that place was called The Valley of Berachah until this day. Then they returned, every man of Judah and Jerusalem, with Jehoshaphat in front of them, to go back to Jerusalem with joy, for the Lord had made them rejoice over their enemies. So they came to Jerusalem, with stringed instruments and harps and trumpets, to the house of the Lord. And the fear of God was on all the kingdoms of those countries when they heard that the Lord had fought against the enemies of Israel. Then the realm of Jehoshaphat was quiet, for his God gave him rest all around."

2 Chronicles 20:23-30

The intention of the enemy was to take Judah captive and place all the inhabitants under a perpetual bondage. The God who sits on the throne ruled against the enemies as the voice of praise and worship of Jehoshaphat and his people resounded from His throne. The enemies foolishly came to battle with abundance of riches and this became treasures to the givers of praise. Prior to the commencement of the battle, sacrifice of praise was placed before the throne. As the battle came in full force, praise soaked the throne of God and the aftermath of the battle was

Black

again witnessed by another round of praise in Jerusalem away from the battlefield.

Let me conclude this chapter by admonishing that if the Ammonites and the Amorites of this world write a letter of threat to you just like they did to Jehoshaphat and Judah in the days of the Bible, do not hesitate to gather your instruments of praise, send your response to the throne of judgement as praise and leave the rest for the God who sits on the throne of judgement to determine the enemies' faith. I congratulate you well ahead of the outstanding victory and uncommon testimonies that are coming your way as you take a clue from Jehoshaphat and the people of Judah.

Chapter 8

PRAISE - A DOOR OPENER

Chapter 8

PRAISE - A DOOR OPENER

Traveling a long journey either by air or road has always been one of the things I enjoy doing most for vacations and carrying out God's assignments. The road accident I shared in Chapter Six happened during one of those journeys, and someone who is completely ignorant of the power of praise may tend to back off, reduce his assignments of the kingdom and conclude that enough is enough having experienced such a terrible incident.

Sometimes ago, we embarked on a journey that would last for more than five hours on the road for an important assignment. The location is better reached by road to avoid driving another three hours from the nearest airport and I had to drive for our convenience. My wife and I embarked on the first segment of the journey which lasted for like seven hours more than the scheduled time due to road constructions and unexpected traffic gridlocks on the way. Thankfully, we were still able to meet up and had a very successful program courtesy of a very close Church Officer and family friend.

The following day, we set out very early in the morning to beat some of the setbacks we had encountered the previous day along with a sister who also attended the function. The car stereo was at its best, giving a perfect mixed sound of praise and we all in one accord sang along with the presence of the Lord of hosts felt everywhere. Though the journey was so smooth that we hardly spent up to five hours before we arrived at our destination, there were two strange occurrences like the fiery darts which God of heaven quenched by His fire! While approaching the Redemption Camp along Lagos – Ibadan expressway in the South Western part of Nigeria through Ibadan axis, a lame man crawling across the road suddenly appeared in the middle of the road from God knows where. Anyone conversant with that road would ask what and how could a lame man be found in that section of the road? It was like a mirage to everyone in the Car. The unexpected happened! There was a sudden door of escape which can still not be explained by anyone; but remember, everyone was soaked in praises to God right from the beginning of the journey. When a man submits to the praise of heavens, an unusual door of deliverance and safety is prepared against every enslavement and enclosure of the devil. Bloodthirsty demons are fed with the blood of Jesus as praise goes to God and they become miserably powerless. It was a great deliverance and all we could see was just a miracle.

As if that was not enough, as we were getting closer home, pains that almost saw me out crawling out of the car came from nowhere. I was practically assisted to climb through the steer-case to my flat and I could only sit quietly on the carpet in the living room. The devil tried harder to inject spirit of fear into us, rather than succumb, my wife and I became more aggressive singing to God in tongues as the kingdom of God suffers violence and only the violent take it by force. My daughter quickly brought the anointing oil on my request, anointed my head and took a few drops into my mouth, suddenly I felt like using the restroom, but the fear of being assisted came calling while I struggled to get on my feet…... The manifestation of God's power was seen raw as the healing was instant and like a dream. … I had to stand before God to testify of His power the following day in church being Sunday.

Have you ever wondered why God called David a man after His own heart? He will never enter the presence of God without first sending His praise!

> ***"Enter into his gates with thanksgiving, and into his courts with praise: be thankful unto him, and bless his name. " "For the LORD is good; his mercy is everlasting, and his truth endureth to all generations. "***
>
> ***Psalm 100:4, 5***

Have you ever misplaced a key to your car or come across someone who lost a key to his apartment? All other activities will come to a standstill, as the key issue must be sorted out. When a Christian is approaching the throne of grace, there could be so many issues to get sorted before God, but the best form of approach and the very first thing is to offer Him praise. When you offer God praise, you make your case easy to evaluate and resolve. Praise opens the door as you approach God and it is not out of place to say that praise is a password or the key that ensures express access and permission into His sanctuary.

We once declared all Sundays in a month as covenant Sundays of celebration, thanksgiving, and praise. It was amazing all that God did before that month came to an end. Expectations were met beyond our imaginations as forgotten and unexpected letters of benefits were delivered; status change and a whole lot were just dropping at members doors. It was a season of celebration and God using the praises offered by His people as door openers to great things.

> ***"And the multitude rose up together against them: and the magistrates rented off their clothes and commanded to beat [them]. And when they had laid many stripes upon them, they cast [them] into prison, charging the jailor to keep them safely: Who, having received such a charge, thrust them into the inner prison, and made their feet fast in the stocks. And at midnight Paul and Silas prayed, and sang praises unto God: and the prisoners heard them. And suddenly there was a great earthquake so that the foundations of the prison were shaken: and immediately all the doors were opened, and every one's bands were loosed. And the keeper of the prison awaking out of his sleep, and seeing the prison doors open, he drew out his sword and would have killed himself,***

supposing that the prisoners had been fled." Act 16:16, 22-27 KJV

Paul and Silas turned their pain to praise and the gain of freedom came calling. Hardly can praise be discussed without referencing the exploit of Paul and Silas in the prison. The story is however so popular and so clear that the possibility of forgetting the Rhema behind the testimony is high. The humiliation and thorough beating received by Paul and Silas were enough to discourage them from rising to their feet.

These Missionaries suffered for sharing the gospel as their freedom was taken away, their primary concern while in prison would have been a fight for freedom, but they focused on connecting to God via praise. Praise did not just open the gate of the prison, but also opened the heart of the prison keeper and was at the mercy of the prisoners. Those that turn their prayers to praise while waiting on the Lord, their offering of praise has the capacity to do more than what they may be bargaining for.

"But they that wait upon the LORD shall renew [their] strength; they shall mount up with wings as eagles; they shall run, and not be weary; [and] they shall walk, and not faint Isa 40:31 KJV

Here comes the challenge to you who is privileged to be reading this right now... If your normal routine is praying and fasting while waiting upon the Lord either during your personal time of prayers or at the usual general waiting of your local church, let praise, appreciation, and thanksgiving take a larger chunk of your waiting time and let praise sort out your needs and open the door of His blessings.

If thanksgiving is the will of God as declared by the Apostle Paul in 1 Thessalonians 1:18, I feel so strongly that fulfilling the will of God may never be accomplished if praise is not involved. In thanksgiving, divine goodness is embraced and celebrated, and this can only happen by acknowledging the Giver and the Owner of everything which is no one but God. Our period of waiting should be our time of praising.

> ***"And to the angel of the church in Philadelphia write; These things saith he that is holy, he that is true, he that hath the key of David, he that openeth, and no man shutteth; and shutteth, and no man openeth; I know thy works: behold, I have set before thee an open door, and no man can shut it: for thou hast a little strength, and hast kept my word, and hast not denied my name."***
>
> ***Rev 3:7-8 KJV***

Christ is the head of the Church and He himself has the key of David. Is it not thought-provoking that out of so many notable characters in the old and new covenants, the Bible distinguished and referenced David and that the key of the kingdom has a link with the name? Looking at the human genealogy of our Lord and Saviour Jesus Christ in chapter one of the book of Matthew, the genealogy was traced from Abraham to Joseph the Carpenter making about fourty one generations, but we have the Bible talking about the key of David and not any other name.

Philadelphia was one of the seven churches in Asia in the book of Revelations. It is amazing that the Church has the highest praise above all other churches and was the modest and most spiritual. One of God's rewards or promises for their faithful living was to give them the key of David and open doors.

Why the key of David? The qualities found in the life of David were also seen revolving around the Philadelphia Church. Though we may say that David was down a few moments in his life, he would however always rise with the little strength in him to please God and fearfully serve Him. His commitment to God in carrying out his primary assignments to God is without prejudice and would not even succumb to mockery from anyone including his wife – Michal in (2 Samuel 6:14 -23)

"So David and all the house of Israel brought up the ark of the LORD with shouting, and with the sound of the trumpet. ... Then David returned to bless his household. And Michal the daughter of Saul came out to meet David, and said, How glorious was the king of Israel to day, who uncovered himself to day in the eyes of the handmaids of his servants, as one of the vain fellows shamelessly uncovereth himself! And David said unto Michal, [It

was] before the LORD, which chose me before thy father, and before all his house, to appoint me ruler over the people of the LORD, over Israel: therefore will I play before the LORD."

2 Samuel 6:15, 20-21 KJV

David, a man of praise, never hesitated to give Michal the right answer beyond her expectations. My understanding is that, God using David to replace Saul the father of Michal, was enough to explain that Saul lost the throne because he was a self-praise seeker who departed from the will and way of the Lord.

The key of David is a reference to a life of his truthfulness and the desire to always have God present with him. Hardly will David embark on any journey or battle without inquiring from God and asking for His backing. Just as David meant so much to God, so also was the Philadelphia church, and the name David eventually became more or less like a household name in His kingdom and in life to come.

If you have your praise, you have a place in God's heart and if you can find a place in God's heart, you can be sure that He will suffer no man to do you any wrong and will always reproof kings for your sake with the instruction that you are untouchable as God's own prophet of praise. If your praise finds a place for you in God's heart, all ancient gates will give way, while the doors of uncommon levels will continually be opened before you.

"He suffered no man to do them wrong: yea, he reproved kings for their sakes; [Saying], Touch not mine anointed, and do my prophets no harm."

Psalm 105:14-15 KJV

To every territory, kingdom, city, nation or town, apart from physical gates that you may see with your eyes, there are always spiritual gates granting or denying human access. Spiritual gates and doors should be under your control if only you know how to engage your instrument of praise! The children of Israel engaged the instrument of praise against the wall of Jericho and it answered to their command.

Chapter 9

INSTRUMENTS OF PRAISE

Chapter 9

INSTRUMENTS OF PRAISE

No matter how beautifully designed a car may look like; a driver is still needed to move and control it. If the latest jet can fly or travel at the speed of light, basically, a Pilot is still required to sit on the Pilot cabin of the jet or airplane to fly it. The most important instrument of praise to God is the Church and when we say the church it means the body of Christ as long as Jesus rules and reigns in such hearts in which you belong if you already have Jesus in your life.

> *Eph 5:15-19 KJV*
> ***"See then that ye walk circumspectly, not as fools, but as wise, Redeeming the time, because the days are evil. Wherefore be ye not unwise but understanding what the will of the Lord [is]. And be not drunk with wine, wherein is excess; but be filled with the Spirit; 19 Speaking to yourselves in psalms and hymns and spiritual songs, singing and making melody in your heart to the Lord;"***

From the preceding chapters of this book, we have been able to show examples of Men who praised and worship God in different situations; they were simply doing the needful - making melody to God from their heart. The letter written by Paul the Apostle in Ephesians above, lay emphasis on the need to quickly assume the position of a melody maker to God; knowing well that humans are the instrument of His praise. Time and tide wait for no man and the evil of the day is enough for the day, not behaving as naïve or people with little or no knowledge who do not understand the benefits of making melody or praising God. He further admonished that Praise is a thing of the heart, a reality requiring our urgent attention.

Why would you say you are not qualified to worship and praise Him? Here what God says:

1Corinthians 1:27 KJV

"But God hath chosen the foolish things of the world to confound the wise; and God hath chosen the weak things of the world to confound the things which are mighty;"

Psalm 8:2 KJV

"Out of the mouth of babes and sucklings hast thou ordained strength because of thine enemies, that thou mightiest still the enemy and the avenger."

Rom 8:1 KJV

"[There is] therefore now no condemnation to them which are in Christ Jesus, who walk not after the flesh, but after the Spirit."

As earlier mentioned, if you have been cleansed by the blood, you are automatically qualified to be God's instrument of praise. God is not searching for Men of wisdom to be instruments of praise as He uses the foolish things of this world to confound the wise. All it takes is humility and willingness to bow before His throne. From the mouth of babes and sucklings he ordained strength which another version of the Bible interpreted as Praise. Therefore no one is too young to praise or too new in faith to be God's own instrument of praise.

Psalm 150:6 KJV
"Let everything that hath breath praise the LORD. Praise ye the LORD."

Rev 5:13 KJV
"And every creature which is in heaven, and on the earth, and under the earth, and such as are in the sea, and all that are in them, heard I saying, Blessing, and honour, and glory, and power, [be] unto him that sitteth upon the throne, and unto the Lamb for ever and ever."

Another instrument of praise in God's hand is EVERYTHING that has breath including man. Praise the Lord! Man was privileged to be man in God's hand and was created to dominate the earth; if man does not understand animal languages, God does! However, if we critically pick a domestic animal like dogs for instance and most especially the trained ones, they understand signs and words of command and I can emphatically say that sounds of songs will not be strange to them. In their own way, they will be giving praise to their maker who remains the great God. When the Bible says everything that has breath, it has no exemption; the six categories of animals represented in Science (Invertebrates, Fish, Amphibians, Reptiles, Birds and Mammals) including plants are all creatures with breath.

If you are fortunate to be created a man, and you also come across this book, just visualize how much praise you owe God and be prepared to give all to Him. I will quickly give you two reasons why you must pay your debt of praise for God not to have created you as a lower animal, invertebrates, reptiles or what have you.

If you were created to be a lower animal, you probably would have been sacrificed or used as a sacrificial offering without any litigation or anyone querying the reason why.

If you were made a lower animal, you would still have praised God as instructed by God and possibly still be killed either for eating purposes or for other reasons.

At this point, I hope you now understand why God invested so much in your making as man whose sole and primary responsibility is to worship God!

God Almighty created you from the dust of the ground and released His breath upon you, making you a Higher Being! You were originally an ordinary dust, but He needed your worship and praise hence breathe upon you. Will you be His instrument of praise? Think about it...

Now, going to other instruments of praise, it is of the belief that since hardly did the Bible mention any other instrument of praise in the new testament to worship apart from singing and making melody in our hearts to God, there should not be any of such instruments mentioned in the old testament to praise Him under the dispensation of grace. In my opinion, this is a doctrinal interpretation of the Bible which I think was also traditionally carved out by some denominations.

There may not be a New Testament church that used musical instruments during the time of the Bible, but there is no condemnation of using instruments to worship. David who skilfully played and pleased God in the Old Testament became God's favourite and a man of God's own heart whom our Lord Jesus came through his lineage as explained in Chapter Eight.

That the Bible is silent on instruments in the New Testament is never an excuse for instruments not to be used. We need to ask the following questions:

Was the use of instruments condemned in any part of the Old Testament?
Was the use beneficial?
Were there signs and wonders when used?
Did God approve of it?
Did it please God?

In aggregate, my answers are Yes! Yes!! And Yes!!!

Most of today's modern technologies in use were somehow not available during the time of the Bible, but we can see them in use for the propagation of the gospel today. Social Media has turned the world into a global village though it has its own effects. We have Gospel Music channels where souls are daily blessed as we sing along, so also old hymnals are now preserved and are soul lifting. Jesus by the lake of Gennesaret used Peter's ship as a podium to comfortably sit and reach the crowd. In today's picnic, the public address system makes the task easier and a broadcast through radio, television stations or any of the Social Media platforms will make the assignment much easier.

Psalm 150:3-5
"Praise him with the sound of the trumpet: praise him with the psaltery and harp. Praise him with the timbrel and dance: praise him with stringed instruments and organs. Praise him upon the loud cymbals: praise him upon the high-sounding cymbals."

Samuel 16:23

"And it came to pass, when the [evil] spirit from God was upon Saul, that David took an ***harp, and played with his hand: so Saul was refreshed, and was well, and the evil spirit departed from him."***

Chronicles 29:25

"And he set the Levites in the house of the LORD with cymbals, with psalteries, and with harps, according to the commandment of David, and of Gad the king's seer, and Nathan the prophet: for [so was] the commandment of the LORD by his prophets."

Can you imagine how boring a church worship will be without any or most of those instruments specifically mentioned and commanded to be used in the Old Testament? We can be sure that these instruments had been improved greatly upon to make music more attractive, interesting and to enhance our worship and praise to God Almighty.

Playing instruments in worship and praise to God brings man's various creativity into attention apart from the beauty it creates. David played for King Saul whenever he was afflicted, and evil spirits will jump out of him.

1Samuel 16:16, 23

"Let our lord now command thy servants, [which are] before thee, to seek out a man, [who is] a cunning player on an harp: and it shall come to pass, when the evil spirit from God is upon thee, that he shall play with his hand, and thou shalt be well. ... And it came to pass, when the [evil] spirit from God was upon Saul, that David took an harp, and played with his hand: so Saul was refreshed, and was well, and the evil spirit departed from him."

If instruments are rightly used, it becomes a two-edged sword of rendering worship to God and becoming a warship to devastate the kingdom of the devil.

We have several places in the scriptures where instructions were given to the children of Israel on how to worship and what instruments to use among which are the following:

Trumpets (Exodus 19:16; 20:18; Leviticus 25:9; Judges 3:27; 1 Kings 1:39; Psalm 150:3 ;)
Flutes (Genesis 4:21; Job 21:12; Psalm 150:4; David 3:5-15;)
Horns (Psalms 98:4-6, Psalms 81:3, Exodus 19:13; 2 Chronicles 15:14),
Harps (Genesis 4:21; 1 Samuel 16:18; Job 30:31; Psalms 43:4; 81:2; 149:3; 150:3; David 3:5-11; Revelation 5:8),

Lyres (Psalms 33:2; 71:22; 81:2; 108:2; 144:9; David 3:5-10),
Cymbals (Psalms 150:1-6; 1 Corinthians 13:1, 2 Samuel 6:5, 1 Chronicles 13:8), and
Tambourines (Psalms 149:3; Isaiah 5:12; see also Genesis 31:27; Exodus 15:20-21; Judges
11:34; 1 Samuel 10:5; 18:6-7; 2 Samuel 6:5, 1 Chronicles 13:8; Job 21:12; Psalms 68:24-25; 81:1-2; 150:4; Isaiah 24:8; 30:32; Jeremiah 31:4).
It will not be right to conclude this chapter by not defining what instrument is. Simply put, Instrument is a device used for a particular purpose. God is the Potter and humans are clay which is like an instrument in His hands. Clay has no say in the hands of the Potter, but to yield to the modeling and carving of the Porter. God has everything it takes to mold you into his taste only if you are willing. To live a purposeful and fulfilled life, you must just see yourself as an instrument or a device that will praise God and that God can willingly and reliably use for His praise.

Jeremiah 18:5-6
Then the word of the LORD came to me, saying, O house of Israel, cannot I do with you as this potter? saith the LORD. Behold, as the clay [is] in the potter's hand, so [are] ye in mine hand, O house of Israel.

Chapter 10

SOUNDS OF PRAISE

Chapter 10

SOUNDS OF PRAISE

The Bible says that out of the abundance of the heart the mouth speaks. In as much as God requires a man coming before His presence to have a clean heart and the right Spirit, the mouth must be ready to express the intent of the heart. Every part of the body has its own function; the mouth will be of no value if it cannot make a sound of praise and a joyful noise unto its Maker as God inhabits the praises of His people. Let me quickly point out here also that the mouth is the gate to the entire body system, therefore; if there must be an access to the throne, the mouth must declare it otherwise such a destiny is shut forever!

Sound is not just an auditory impression that can be perceived by the sense of hearing, but it is also an expression that can be heard and relate with. In praising the Lord, the Psalmist commanded in Psalm 66:8 that we should bless God and make the voice of His praise to be heard. The Melody of your praise to God is as important as the heart you are approaching the throne of Grace with. I offer this prayer for my readers now that your sound of praise shall be melodious to God's hearing and that of men in the name of Jesus and may the sound of your praise not turn to ordinary sound in God's ear. If the sound coming out of your praise is pleasant to

God's ear, it shows a great sign of acceptance to God and I have no single doubt in my heart that the Angels will in one accord praise the Almighty God with it.

Again, we need to come to terms and reason out why God created us. He made us to be instruments with the ability to sing and make music as we saw in chapter ten. The Sound of Praise communicates with God, declares the Glory of God and expresses His wonderful acts.

> *Judges 7:20-23 KJV*
> ***"And the three companies blew the trumpets, and brake the pitchers, and held the lamps in their left hands, and the trumpets in their right hands to blow [withal]: and they cried The sword of the LORD, and of Gideon. And they stood every man in his place round about the camp: and all the host ran, and cried, and fled. And the three hundred blew the trumpets, and the LORD set every man's sword against his fellow, even throughout all the host: and the host fled to Bethshittah in Zererath, [and] to the border of Abelmeholah, unto***
> ***Tabbath. And the men of Israel gathered themselves together out of Naphtali, and out of Asher, and out of all Manasseh, and pursued after the Midianites."***

For every action of praise, there is always an effect and a reaction of sound that follows!

It is only the living that can produce sounds of praise; hence it is a privilege to be used of God. The Israelites did evil before the Lord and God punished them by sending the Amalekites, Midianites and the people of the East along with their camels in hundreds of thousands to waste their labour and ruin their harvest. After repentance, Gideon stood in the gap and trimmed thirty-two thousands of volunteered armies to just three hundred chosen by God's instruction to confront their assailants. Three companies of one hundred armies along with their trumpets surrounded the camp of the intruders. They blew their trumpets! Three hundred trumpets echoed a unique sound of praise to put the enemies on their feet!

How do you feel when you are asked to shout and make a joyful noise unto the Lord either in Church, home or any Christian gathering? Take a look at this scripture -

2Chronicles 5:13

"It came even to pass, as the trumpeters and singers [were] as one, to make one sound to be heard in praising and thanking the LORD; and when they lifted up [their] voice with the trumpets and cymbals and instruments of musick, and praised the LORD, [saying], For [he is] good; for his mercy [endureth] forever:

that [then] the house was filled with a cloud, [even] the house of the LORD;"

Your noise is a sound of praise to God which is one of the fulfilments of your purpose on earth to please and draw God's presence. Your lips are given to you and as well empowered to shout for joy to God, the rock of your salvation because of His deliverance as declared in Psalm 71:23 and Psalm 95:1. If you are living right with God, your shout produces a sound of His praise and you can now begin to imagine when God is happy receiving your shout and sound of praise how the enemy will be terrified! Common give the Lord a shout!

It is scriptural to shout! It is an act of worship to produce sound of praise as God awaits our new songs every time and anytime we come into His presence. It is abnormal to keep quiet when we are to offer God shouts, it is never a sign of purity or holiness, but a mere wrong interpretation of the scriptures and its injunctions - We are not in the cemetery or in the mortuary, but in the sanctuary of praise to our God. The Bible cannot be broken and may I emphasize that shout has no other interpretation or any other meaning other than shout! Common give the Lord a shout and let me repeat that God gave this instruction in Psalm 95:1.

Psalm 40:3.
"And he hath put a new song in my mouth, [even] praise unto our God: many shall see [it], and fear, and shall trust in the LORD."

Your songs and sounds of praise are medium of expression to both Christians and non-Christians and this will amount to a selfish living if not done. Why? There is a joyful demonstration that comes with the act of making a sound of praise to God which others are expected to see. In the course of seeing you praise your God, their heart is turned to God, bringing the fear of God upon such souls in repentance and making them trust in Him. This is just the simple interpretation of the above scriptures in Psalm 40.

As we conclude this chapter, let us quickly ponder over this scripture:

Job 32:8
"There is a spirit in man: and the inspiration of the Almighty giveth them understanding."

Every man on earth is kept by the breath or inspiration of the Almighty God and your living is for a purpose. Anytime it comes to your understanding that you have the breath of God in you, take it as another opportunity to join the twenty-four elders in making a resounding Sound of Praise to the Occupier of the throne of glory which is God Himself.

Satan was an angel beautifully created and commissioned by God as the Choir leader in heaven because he had the breath of the Almighty God upon him. He however saw himself in the place of God; he arrogantly contended for the throne of glory and God dethroned, and cast him down. Whereas Lucifer and his fallen angels contended for the throne of glory, the twenty-four elders, the angels and other creatures are presently surrounding this same throne of glory bowing down to God with their pure sound of praise. The devil fought to have the same glory with God, but the elders are still busy praising and singing about the glory of God because they have the breath of the Almighty God upon them.

If the living creatures and elders in heaven right from the days of the Bible have been very busy shouting His glory and singing His praise, and they have not completed the first verse of His hymn of glory, will you not rather join them while on earth to make a resounding noise and shout His praise, so that you can be worthy of singing His praise in heaven through eternity? It is time to understand that singing God's praise is not an option, but an assignment that must be carried out as a primary duty.

Chapter 11

HEALING BALM OF PRAISE

Chapter 11

HEALING BALM OF PRAISE

If you have ever had a doctor's appointment or visited any medical facility; you did, simply because you needed to get some health issues sorted out and you have some trust in the health personnel. There is however a clinic you can visit without any prior appointment for a free consultation, diagnosis and healing at no cost to you. Take a step of faith today, visit a praise clinic and have a divine experience with Jehovah Rapha, the Lord our Healer! You need no one to set this meeting up, but you have everything it takes to start one even right now. Having read through this book; The Audacity of Praise from the beginning, you will agree with me that praise is not only physical but spiritual as well.

When you have an appointment with Jehovah – Rapha through praise, you are calling for His touch and divine healing in all ramifications as He is the I am that I am who is a strong tower that saves the righteous, the praise givers when they run unto Him… (Pro 18:10 - The name of the LORD [is] a strong tower: the righteous runneth into it, and is safe.) Jehovah-Rapha has the power to heal physically:

2Kings 5:10

"And Elisha sent a messenger unto him, saying, Go and wash in Jordan seven times, *and thy flesh shall come again to thee, and thou shalt be clean."*

Psalm 34:19-20

"Many [are] the afflictions of the righteous: but the LORD delivereth him out of them all. 20 He keepeth all his bones: not one of them is broken."

Jehovah -Rapha is the name that heals all emotional complications

Psalm 34:18

"The LORD [is] nigh unto them that are of a broken heart; and saveth such as be of a contrite spirit."

Mental healing is put to flight by the name Jehovah -Rapha

Daniel 4:34

"And at the end of the days I Nebuchadnezzar lifted up mine eyes unto heaven, and mine understanding returned unto me, and I blessed the most

High, and I praised and honoured him that liveth forever, whose dominion [is] an everlasting dominion, and his kingdom [is] from generation to generation:"

Jehovah Rapha is the name that raises standard against all spiritual battles
Psalm 103:2-3
"Bless the LORD, O my soul, and forget not all his benefits: who forgiveth all thine iniquities; who healeth all thy diseases;"

The Purifying and the Healing Power of Jehovah-Rapha is never comparable!

1Corinthians 2:14
"But the natural man receiveth not the things of the Spirit of God: for they are foolishness unto him: neither can he know [them], because they are spiritually discerned."

Praise has become more of a demonstration of faith in God and His ability to do the unimaginable. If faith is defined as the substance of things hoped for and the evidence of things not seen, praise as an instrument of faith makes the impossibility possible with God and I am quite sure that for anyone to be willing to offer God praise, there is a portion of faith attached or a seed of mustard seed-like faith in play, and as many as called upon His name shall be saved! And shall be healed.

Immediately the Israelites got rescued from Egypt and crossed the Red Sea, a reminder came from God through Moses saying:

> *Exodus 15:26 KJV]*
> ***"And said, If thou wilt diligently hearken to the voice of the LORD thy God, and wilt do that which is right in his sight, and wilt give ear to his commandments, and keep all his statutes, I will put none of these diseases upon thee, which I have brought upon the Egyptians: for I [am] the LORD that healeth thee."***

What is the voice of the Lord and what does diligently hearkening to His voice entails? You will recall that in Chapter three, we explained that God had to kill the first born of the Egyptians and drowned Pharaoh and his cohort in the red sea because they presented themselves as obstacles to the worship God demanded from the Israelites. The voice and the command of God is doing His will, living right to declare His worship and praising Him for Who He is, and then our healing is assured.

At the beginning of every winter in Maryland, United States of America and other states too, there used to be a health campaign program and a shot against flu with other winter related health diseases for individuals to put preventive measures in place. The spiritual medicine needed to put preventive measures in place against any of the diseases of the Egyptians as demanded by God is simply hearkening to His word, obeying His instructions and you will but live to reap divine health as you live to worship and give God your praise.

Don Moen, a seasoned wrong writer and a worship leader corroborated the name of God as Jehovah Rapha in his song that says:

> ***"I am the Lord that healeth thee, I am the Lord your Healer, I sent my word and I heal your diseases, I am the Lord your Healer … "***

Yes indeed! He is the Lord that heals us from all our infirmities. We cannot deny the fact that a whole lot of diseases, infirmities, and viruses are on a rampage these days; spiritual illnesses, emotional breakdown, physical health challenges, and many more, but there is a balm of healing that many are failing to explore! There is a balm of healing in your praise and worship.

Several years back, I was a Fellowship Pastor on Campus but needed to be healed of emotional and psychological trauma of having had to carry over a pre-requisite course from my first year to the third year in the University. I failed the subject because I underestimated and took it for granted during my first year while I had distinctions and grade B in others. It was so disturbing and hurting that I failed the subject again and again till I got serious with it in year three. I came to my senses one day and had to employ the healing balm of worship and praise on my knees. Thereafter, it was quite surprising that I suddenly became a teacher to other course mates, I sat for the exam and it was like a dream when I eventually got a good grade in it. This testimony perhaps simply explains what Apostle Paul says in ***1Corinthinas 1: 18 through 19 KJV: "For the preaching of the cross is to them that perish foolishness; but unto us which are saved it is the power of God. For it is written, I will destroy the wisdom of the wise, and will bring to nothing the understanding of the prudent". I sincerely pray that your mind of understanding shall be enlightened to see and know that there is a balm of healing in your worship and praise to God. When your spirit and soul come alive, your entire system will be awakened to greater exploits.***

1Samuel 16:14-17, 21-23

"But the Spirit of the LORD departed from Saul, and an evil spirit from the LORD troubled him. And Saul's servants said unto him, Behold now, an evil spirit from God troubleth thee. Let our lord now command thy servants, [which are] before thee, to seek out a man, [who is] a cunning player on an harp: and it shall come to pass, when the evil spirit from God is upon thee, that he shall play with his hand, and thou shalt be well. And Saul said unto his servants, Provide me now a man that can play well, and bring [him] to me. ...

> ***And David came to Saul, and stood before him: and he loved him greatly; and he became his armour bearer. And Saul sent to Jesse, saying, Let David, I pray there, stand before me; for he hath found favour in my sight. And it came to pass, when the [evil] spirit from God was upon Saul, that David took an harp, and played with his hand: so Saul was refreshed, and was well, and the evil spirit departed from him."***

From the above scriptures, it was made clear that David's skilful playing of the musical instrument was a therapy to King Saul. Are you a gifted worship and praise Leader? Let me declare to you that souls are waiting to be healed at the sound of your praise! Will you kind-heartedly put away pride and arrogance to attend to the souls that needed to be revived and brought back to life by listening to you sing?

There are so many people gifted in playing musical instruments like David of old, but they cannot hearken to a call that will not yield any profit into their pockets. David was recommended by one of King Saul's protocol officers, he responded without asking for part payment in advance and neither did David refer Saul's messenger to see and negotiate with his personal assistance or his Manager before giving attention to the messenger of the King. That was David's first encounter with the throne of kingship in Israel and he eventually took over the throne by divine appointment.

Oh yes! it is true that a man's gift makes a way for him and may I request not to be misinterpreted as I explain further. We must and should be willing to put profit behind us and reach out to souls that are dying because their souls lack remedy of songs to live and survive. Thank God for all our renowned and well-known gospel ministers, most especially those who are sponsoring the gospel with their own resources seeking for the kingdom of God first and healing souls via the balm in their worship and praise.

Let me conclude this book and this chapter with a very short story I saw on a social media about a blind little boy who was out begging in the street for survival which we were encouraged to share as well. He had a signboard by his side which reads "Please help me, I am a blind poor boy" people barely noticed the board and he could hardly earn some coins, though it was a busy corner of the street. At the middle of the day, a man crossed by him and noticed that board; he stopped by the poor boy and threw some coins in his hat. He did not only give him some coins but changed the words on the board.

A few moments later, the blind boy was surprised that a lot of coins were coming in his hat with so many people noticing that boy and trying to help him. The boy was amazed and wanted to know the reason for the sudden turning point. The following day, the man who changed the inscription on his board stopped by him to see if there is a change in the condition of the poor boy. Though the poor boy was blind, he was able to recognize his footsteps and he asked him, "What did you do yesterday?" The man just smiled and said I made a little change on your signboard. The boy asked further, what was the change you made? "Today is a beautiful day and I

can't see it" The boy said, "But the meaning is the same, which made the people help me more than the usual?" The man told him, "Yes you are right, but the first sign simply told them that you are blind. "The second sign made them aware that they weren't blind" The boy now understood it very well. The story concluded with the following words ...
Always help someone – You might be the only one that does
Do well for others – It will come back in unexpected ways

Hear what the Bible says:
Pro 29:18 KJV
"Where [there is] no vision, the people perish: but he that keepeth the law, happy [is] he."

Your vision is not just for you alone but also is your song and your ideas! There are some that are waiting to be healed by your awaited worship and praise! Just like the little poor blind boy, someone is waiting for the balm of healing from you and would you not rather see audacity of praise as call for action from your end? God bless you and thank you for reading.

FINAL WORD

Your praise is a mighty force that pulls down and a strong component that builds up. It is an arrow of offence and destruction to your enemies while it serves as a wall of defense to anyone who offers praise to God. If you want to be fully equipped for battle, you must be willing and ever ready to put the whole armour of your Praise on!

Your praise can turn your scarcity to surplus and bring devastating consequences to anyone who dares your God!

You may probably have read other books on various subjects of praise by other notable writers, be rest assured that Audacity of Praise is fully inspired and loaded with great and powerful revelations of how faster and farther your praise travels whenever you give it to God. I encourage you to pick up this lovely book, get copies for your friends and recommend it for others.

Do not underrate your praise as it boosts and rates your rank higher before God; and it travels farther when you are not far from God in praise.